Tip-top

TEAS

Great Britain's top 100 tea rooms

Laura Harper

foreword by Jane Pettigrew

studio **cactus**

First published in Great Britain in 2003 by

studio**cactus** ltd

13 SOUTHGATE STREET   WINCHESTER   HAMPSHIRE   SO23 9DZ
TEL 01962 878600   FAX 01962 850209   ISDN 01962 859277
E-MAIL MAIL@STUDIOCACTUS.CO.UK   WEBSITE WWW.STUDIOCACTUS.CO.UK

Copyright © 2003 studio**cactus** ltd
Text Copyright © Laura Harper
Photographs © 2003 studio**cactus** ltd
ISBN 1-904239-01-3

A catalogue record for this book is
available from the British Library.

Printed in Singapore by Imago

Contents

Foreword

It is ironic that it was in coffee houses that tea was first offered to the English public in the 1660s. In the 1880s, however, the fashion for coffee gave way to a new trend for tea houses, the first being set up by the Aerated Bread Company some time in 1884. The chain of ABC bakery shops and tea rooms was so successful that other companies copied the idea and before long there were tea rooms all over Britain.

In rural Britain, cottage tea rooms became popular when the fashion for country walking and cycling encouraged people out of the noisy, smoky towns and into the fresh air and green countryside. Of course, such outings were never complete without a pot of tea and a bun in a little village teashop. Gradually, going out to tea became an essential part of British social life, and although some of the best venues disappeared in the 1950s and 60s when instant coffee first grabbed

Tea as it should be made

Fill the kettle with freshly drawn cold water and set it to boil. When nearly boiling, pour a little water into the pot, swill around, tip away and then measure the tea into the pot. Allow approximately 2.5g for each cup to be brewed. Pour the water onto the leaves as it comes to a rolling boil, then put the lid on the pot and leave to infuse; generally speaking, large-leafed tea needs 3–4 minutes, while smaller particles of leaf need 2–3 minutes. Be careful not to overbrew the tea as it can develop an unpleasant bitter taste. Serve with milk and sugar to taste.

public attention, there are still excellent examples of the perfect English tea room around the country – as this book proves. The very best offer a range of good quality, speciality, loose-leaf teas from the major producing countries of the world, and a selection of lunch and tea-time treats to suit everyone. But, there is more to a favourite teashop than the strength and flavour of the brew and the soft freshness of the scone as it melts in the mouth with its generous dollop of thick, rich clotted cream and delicious, fruity home-made jam. What makes a teashop truly unforgettable is the warm welcome, the attention to detail, and the care and thought that goes in to looking after every single customer. It's a fusion of all those elements that draws people back, again and again, to enjoy our very British tradition of afternoon tea.

How to make traditional scones

Makes 10-12

225g (8oz) self-raising flour

A pinch of salt

50g (2oz) butter, softened

25g (1oz) caster sugar

1 medium egg, beaten

75ml (3fl oz) milk or natural yoghurt

Beaten egg or milk to glaze scones

Heat the oven to 230ºC (450ºF/gas mark 8). Grease a baking tray and dredge with flour. Mix together the flour and salt and rub in the butter as lightly as possible with the fingertips. Stir in the sugar, add the beaten egg and bind together with a fork. Add enough milk or yoghurt to give a stiff dough and knead gently until smooth. Turn the dough out onto a floured board and roll to a thickness of 1in (2.5cm). Cut into circles using a 2.5in (6cm) cutter dipped in flour. Place the scones, almost touching, on the prepared baking tray and brush the tops with beaten egg or milk. Bake for 12–15 minutes until well risen and golden. Remove from the oven and immediately cover with a clean tea cloth to keep the steam in. Serve warm with clotted cream and jam.

Jane Pettigrew, Tea Specialist

Author's introduction

Where would we be without that great British institution, the teashop? Think of the times when all you've wanted is a really good cuppa in a comforting or reviving place, and what a relief when you've found it. But what a letdown when you didn't find what you were looking for. Thankfully there are still plenty of great teashops around the country, doing their bit to help us feel good. But which is your favourite, or your latest worthy find?

With the invaluable help of the British public I have gathered here 100 of the best teashops in Britain. Through the medium of local radio I was

able to send out requests to listeners, encouraging them to nominate their favourite shops, which I later visited in order to pick out the best. Since this is a subjective guide, you may find that your own favourite is missing, but please feel free to contact me through the publishers (see details opposite) and I shall be happy to consider your choice for inclusion in the second edition.

6

By way of apology to those living in Ireland (where I know they have some excellent teashops), I'd like to explain that for this first edition it was not feasible for us to cross the water. However, we intend to expand this book in later editions, so please send in your recommendations. To those readers in Scotland and Wales I should also like to explain that we limited our choice of teashops in your areas to a modest number simply because of restrictions on research time. However, we hope to be able to include greater numbers in subsequent editions of the book.

It has been an enormous pleasure travelling around Britain and meeting the owners (or managers) of so many top-class establishments. I'd like to thank all of them for the warm welcome they give to all their customers and for bearing with me while I collected the necessary information for this book. It was heart-warming to meet so many people who are genuinely enthusiastic about what they do and who put so much sheer effort into it. And without a doubt it's the people running a teashop that make the difference. You can have the prettiest building and the best tea and food, but without that something extra from those in charge things can fall apart. I found in each of the teashops I've included that clear guidance from the top created a consistently welcoming and pleasing place to be. Long live the teashop.

Laura Harper

Contact us at:

studio cactus ltd

13 SOUTHGATE STREET WINCHESTER HAMPSHIRE SO23 9DZ

E-MAIL: MAIL@STUDIOCACTUS.CO.UK

www.tiptopguides.co.uk

Healthy Drinking

Tea is good for you. This has been widely accepted for centuries, but more recent research can tell us why – tea contains a number of vitamins and minerals. It has been proved to contain calcium, zinc (essential for growth and development), folic acid, riboflavin (B2) and vitamins B1 and B6. Also present are manganese (essential for bone growth and the body's development) and potassium (vital for maintaining fluid balance and a normal heartbeat). Tea also helps to top up our daily fluid intake, something we're regularly being reminded to do. Furthermore, all types of tea also contain flavonoids (or antioxidants), which offer protection against major illnesses like cancer and heart disease.

Tea

A potted history

The first shipments of tea imported to Europe were brought by the Dutch and Portuguese in the late 16th and early 17th centuries. Despite the popularity of tea drinking among the upper classes from then onwards, it was not until the early 19th century that tea became widely available to the public at large, thanks to reduced taxation on the commodity. Throughout the Victorian period tea became a focal point of social life for everyone, and teashops grew more and more popular. In Glasgow, for example, a stylish chain was opened around the turn of the 20th century by Stuart Cranston and his sister, Kate (*see* pp.146–149), promoting the best interior designers of the day. The arrival of the tango from Argentina in 1910 spurred a craze among the fashionable set for afternoon tea dances in plush hotels. Despite threats from coffee from the 1960s on, and a reputation for being old-fashioned, teashops never really went away. New establishments began to open in the 1980s and visitors from the US and Japan started taking an interest in British tea. Today, despite tough competition from coffee and soft drinks, tea is once more firmly established as Britain's favourite beverage, and the teashop goes from strength to strength.

Maid at work preparing afternoon tea
1926

Afternoon tea at the Plaza Café, a pavement café in Neath, South Wales
circa May 1936

What is tea?

Tea is simply the leaf from the tea plant, *Camellia sinensis*, a flowering evergreen shrub that grows in many countries around the world. In cultivation, the height of the tea plant is restricted to about 1m (3ft). The soil and climate have a deep impact on the quality of the tea, as do the timing and the method of the picking of the leaves, which is still mostly done by hand. When harvested, the leaves are still green.

The main tea suppliers to the UK are India, Kenya, Sri Lanka (Ceylon), Indonesia, Malawi, Rwanda, Tanzania, Bangladesh, and Mozambique. In the UK, we import more tea than all of Europe and North America combined, and every day we consume about 165 million cups – roughly three per person. Virtually all our tea is blended, meaning it's a mixture of different teas from different countries, whether it's loose-leaf or teabag. Blending allows tea merchants to ensure a consistent colour and flavour at a stable price, since the world's supply of tea (and its prices) are continually changing. Also, some teas do not make a good drink on their own and are better suited to a mix. A teabag might contain 20 or more different types of tea and, of course, it's only as good as the tea that goes into it. Some estates (usually made up of many hundreds or thousands of acres) produce such good quality tea that it can be drunk on its own, rather than blended. These are called single-estate teas and you will find them at several of the teashops in this guide.

In the making of black tea (the most commonly found tea), the leaves go straight from the fields to the nearby tea factory and undergo five main processes – withering; rolling or cutting; fermentation (also known as oxidation); drying or firing; and sorting (or grading). In the first stage, much of the moisture is removed by spreading the leaves on racks and blowing warm, dry air over them until they wither. Next the leaves are torn, cut and curled into tiny bits, which releases the juices. This produces the tiny tealeaves that we see in most of the tea drunk in Britain. Alternatively, the leaves are rolled, keeping the leaf larger and producing the finest flavours. During fermentation

What's your cup of tea?

Most teashops offer a standard tea blend or one that has been made specially for them, plus a choice of speciality teas. Of these, the ones you're most likely to find are Assam, Darjeeling, Earl Grey and Lapsang Souchong. Decaffeinated tea is also widely available for those limiting their caffeine intake. The main groups of speciality teas are:

Assam Strong, deep-coloured teas from northern India with a rich, smooth and malty flavour.

Darjeeling Light, delicate teas from the foothills of the Himalayas. Known as the 'champagne of teas'.

Ceylon Strong, highly flavoured teas with a bright colour.

China A huge variety of teas, the best known being the Keemuns (light and delicate black tea) and the wood-smoked Lapsang Souchong (large-leaved black tea).

East Africa Full-bodied and bright copper-coloured teas, most of which end up in teabags.

Green teas Very delicate, mainly from China and Japan, often slightly bitter. Gunpowder is one of the most popular, a refreshing pale-coloured and very light tea.

Fruit teas Tea that is flavoured with fruit pieces or essences.

Fruit/herbal infusions Do not contain any actual tea, being made of fruit or herbal mixtures.

Blends The best known are English Breakfast (full-strength) and Earl Grey (a mix of Keemun and Darjeeling scented with bergamot).

Jasmine A green tea mixed with jasmine flowers.

Nilgiri Black teas from the Nilgiri hills in southern India – bright, fruity and full of flavour.

Pouchong Lightly oxidized China tea with a very mild, smooth flavour and pale golden colour.

the leaf is spread out and left until it changes from green to a bright copper colour. Next, the tea is dried by hot air and then it is sorted into different grades according to leaf size.

In the making of green tea (most of which comes from China), the leaves are not withered but instead are steamed, rolled and fired. Steaming prevents fermentation, and moisture is removed by repeated rolling and firing. As a result the leaf retains its green hue.

Somewhere between a black tea and a green tea is Oolong (from China's Fujian province and Taiwan), which is partially withered and semi-fermented, producing a delicate flavour from an amber or pale golden tea on brewing.

Accompaniments to tea

Many of the best teashops make the most of the local produce available and include it in their recipes. This might be fruit and vegetables, cream or free-range eggs from local farms, organic ingredients, or locally made preserves and chutneys.

As well as tea, today's teashops usually serve coffee, of good quality and served by the cup or in a cafetière from a choice of beans. Some even roast and grind their own. Where coffee is served especially well, I have said so. Hot chocolate is another regular teashop option.

Most teashops have comprehensive menus, usually serving from morning (and often including breakfast) through lunch until late afternoon. Menus are often enhanced by daily specials and local specialities. Where a teashop makes a special effort for vegetarians, we have used the vegetarian symbol to highlight this.

For many people, the quality of a teashop is directly proportional to the standard of the cakes and scones that it sells. I have done my best to seek out teashops that excel at either, or both (and most, if not all of the food, must be home-made). Then there's the cream tea, an adventure in itself, varying in size and ingredients from one part of the country to the next – clotted cream in one county, whipped cream in another. Occasionally it will still be served with delicious home-made jam. If that's not enough for you then afternoon tea awaits, almost a meal in itself. On top of all that, you can enjoy a multitude of regional variations, whether you're on the lookout for savouries or sweets.

Taking tea in London

The capital is known more for its afternoon teas served in smart hotels or department stores than for independent teashops. Since I have aimed to promote the independents, I have not included hotels or big stores here. In London, I have listed a couple of worthwhile teashops – or, rather, one in central London (just off Kensington High Street) and one opposite Kew Gardens, which is really Surrey, but near enough.

Opening hours and phone numbers

Due to the seasonal nature of the teashop business, many establishments have varying opening hours. For example, most are closed over Christmas, but some are open on Boxing Day. The opening times listed in this book are merely general business hours and we advise that you call ahead before setting out to visit any of the featured teashops. Phone numbers can be found in the index on page 156.

The Tea Council and the Tea Guild

The Tea Council is an independent body dedicated to promoting the beverage for the benefit of those who produce, sell and enjoy tea around the world.

Establishments in the UK that meet the Council's highest standards in both preparing and serving tea are invited annually to join the Tea Guild. Teashops featured in this book with the logo shown above are Tea Guild members. The full list of members can be found on the Tea Council website: www.tea.co.uk

How to become a Tea Guild member

All establishments must pass an initial inspection by acknowledged industry tea tasters. Once an outlet has become a member the Tea Council maintains a watching brief throughout the year to ensure that standards of excellence are maintained.

Symbols used in this book

Loose-leaf tea	Teabags	V Vegetarian food options
Fruit tea	Herbal tea	
Non-smoking	Licensed teashop	BH Open on bank holidays

"I'd rather have a cup of tea than go to bed
with someone – any day."

Boy George, 1983

Southern England

Flying Fifteens

19a The Esplanade, Lowestoft, Suffolk

May–end Sept, Tues–Sun (and bank holiday Mondays) 10.30am–5pm. Hours vary with seasons

 V **BH**

Set on Lowestoft's vibrant seafront, Flying Fifteens is named after a class of racing boat designed in the 1940s, and still popular worldwide today. The tea room inhabits an airy elegant villa of the mid-1800s, blessed with high ceilings and French windows looking

straight out to sea. It was built by Sir Samuel Morton Peto, who developed much of 19th-century Lowestoft, and is approached from the pedestrianized Esplanade, or 'Prom' – and through an attractive garden filled with summer flower tubs.

Diana and Peter Knight have run the place since 1996, providing excellent quality at reasonable prices in a

Prince Charles learned to sail on a Flying Fifteen called *Coweslip*, owned by his father. The boats were designed b

18

relaxed atmosphere. Their reputation soon spread by word of mouth, bringing a strong following of locals and holidaymakers.

A major attraction of Flying Fifteens is the excellent selection of loose-leaf teas, mostly supplied by Taylors of Harrogate and offering such exotic varieties as Mountains of the Moon, and Blue Sapphire. The menu describes each tea in detail and 'testers' (glass jars of tea on a pine dresser) can be sniffed to help you choose. Filtered water is used and the more specialized teas are accompanied by an egg timer to encourage sufficient brewing time.

Each day around ten generously sized cakes are displayed, and big meringues are also made daily. The strawberry scones covered with whipped cream and sliced strawberries are a big hit in summer. Savouries include locally smoked salmon, specially prepared for Diana and Peter, and crabs from Cromer. All orders are taken using a numbering system, so make sure you pick up your ticket on arrival.

Uffa Fox and several race out of Lowestoft's yacht club at weekends. Photographs of early boats are displayed in the tea room.

The Tide Mill

The Granary, Tide Mill Way, Woodbridge, Suffolk
Easter–end Sept, Mon & Wed–Sun 10.30am–4.30pm (closed Tues). Hours vary with seasons

Next door to a tourist attraction of the same name, the Tide Mill enjoys a great location in an old granary on the banks of the River Deben. Inside is a relaxing room of bare-bricked walls, tables decked with fresh flowers, and two deep armchairs. This tranquil setting is home to locals and yachtsmen from all over Europe. The welcoming Martin and Imogen Rattle stock an excellent range of fruit and herbal teas, including 'detox' and organics, plus a few speciality black teas. Food consists of imaginative

seasonal dishes, such as fresh crab from nearby Orford, and a modest range of cakes. The coffees are great, the white hot chocolate a delight, and the freshly pressed organic juices delicious.

The Tide Mill next door opens May–Sept, daily 11am–5pm; April & Oct, weekends & bank holidays only 11am–5pm.

The Weavers

2 The Knoll, Peasenhall, near Saxmundham, Suffolk
Daily 9am–5.30pm, all year. Closed Christmas Day and Boxing Day

In a picturesque village on the main tourist route between Stowmarket and Yoxford (the A1120), the Weavers supplies well priced, traditional home-made fare in an intimate setting, using good quality local ingredients. Located at the Sibton end of the village, the teashop has been run for several years by Trudy

Hollands and Andrew Meredith. The menu ranges from all-day breakfasts to cream tea with home-made scones. Several cakes are made daily, and local ham features among the snacks. Celebrity chef Brian Turner once cooked in the Weavers as part of his *Out to Lunch* series, using local bacon smoked in the village.

Saxmundham is in the heart of the Heritage Coast area and only a few miles from the seaside towns of Aldeburgh and Thorpeness.

Poppy's

17 Trinity Street, Colchester, Essex
Mon–Sat 10am–5pm; closed Sun except in December and on Mothering Sunday, 11.30am–2.30pm

The traditional Poppy's offers excellent food in three cosy beamed rooms. Free-range eggs are used in most of the baking and delicious scones are made each morning, including the Fruit Rascal (a fruit and spice version that is great warmed up and served individually or with the cream tea). Poppy's also keeps a

generous supply of freshly made cakes and gateaux as well as offering six traditional afternoon teas to choose from. Meals begin with breakfast and there's a full menu of snacks including focaccia sandwiches, light meals, and daily specials. Lady Grey appears among the speciality teas, while coffee is served by the cup or mug.

Discover Colchester on daily walking tours from June to September. Call the Visitor Information Centre: 01206 282920

The Trinity House Tearoom & Garden

47 High Street, Manningtree, Essex
Mon–Sat 9am–4.30pm. Closed Sunday and bank holidays (but open at Easter)

Manningtree lies on the scenic coastal route between Harwich and Ipswich and near the Essex Way, which is very popular with cyclists and walkers. On the pretty high street is the cheery and relaxed Trinity House, originally built as a vicarage and run for the last decade or

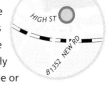

so by Heather and Ray Ablett. Twinings supply the teas, and the teashop is best known for its cakes, pastries and fruit pies,

made in-house and displayed beneath a blackboard listing the daily specials. Why not try the speciality fat-free tea bread? Most of the food is made on the premises, beginning with an all-day breakfast and including vegetarian meals. From the top level of the tiered garden you can catch a glimpse of the River Stour, rich in birdlife.

Trinity House's proceeds are put back in to Acorn Village, a complex that helps adults with learning disabilities.

Tea on the Green

3 Eves Corner, Danbury, Essex
Mon–Fri 8.30am–4.30pm, Sat 10am–4.30pm, Sun 11am–4.30pm. Closed Christmas & New Year

The enormously popular Tea on the Green is a traditional teashop with a contemporary twist. Set opposite the appealing village green in the heart of the community, it gives a sense of space, with fresh decor in an airy room and outdoor tables. Real effort goes into

the good-value food – take your pick from around ten cakes on show, or a daily special such as a pie or flan. While you're at it why not try their generous afternoon tea, presented on a three-tiered cake stand? The savoury menu of snacks and light

meals includes brunch and filled pita breads, plus a daily specials blackboard and a children's menu. Among the speciality teas are Jasmine and Lady Grey, and the coffee is excellent.

Not far away is the beautiful Danbury Country Park, created from the lakeside ornamental gardens of Danbury Palace.

Squires

11 High Street, Rayleigh, Essex
Mon 10am–5pm, Tues–Sat 9am–5pm

Located in a 300-year-old building in the middle of the market town of Rayleigh, Squires is a friendly, traditional teashop with black beams and white walls. There is an excellent variety of loose-leaf teas (served in a glass teapot with its own infuser), and a number of green teas are offered, such as Tea of Life. The range of coffees is also wide, and the food is well presented

and dished out in generous portions. Breakfast, cream tea, and a big afternoon tea are just three menu options. The day's cakes and desserts (around eight in total) include different flavours of the shop's own cheesecake.

The most popular savoury choice is the Squires Special (a toasted muffin served with bacon, tomato and melted cheese).

Lady Foley's

Great Malvern Railway Station, Great Malvern, Worcestershire
April–Sept, Mon–Sat 9am–6pm, Sun 3–6pm; rest of the year, Mon–Sat 9am–6pm (closed Sun)

Hardly what you'd expect to find in a train station these days, Lady Foley's is well worth the visit for its great atmosphere. The station was built in Victorian times and the teashop occupies an impressive room, with William Morris wallpaper on the walls that stretch up to formidably high ceilings. Classical music plays in the

background and bentwood chairs accompany plain dark wooden tables. Extra ironwork tables are set out on the platform. The food is simple and inexpensive and includes home-made cakes as well as a few hot and cold snacks, which can be washed down with a glass of house wine. The tea room is named after a local Victorian lady of the manor.

Designed by local architect Edward Wallace Elmslie, Great Malvern Station remains virtually untouched since its construction in 1863.

The Boston Tea Party

75 Park Street, Bristol, Avon

Mon 7am–6pm, Tues–Sat 7am–10pm, Sun 9am–7pm. Closed Christmas Day and Boxing Day

The trendy, yet good-value Boston Tea Party attracts a stimulatingly bohemian clientele. Built in 1790, this spacious city-centre café serves a delicious range of gourmet sandwiches and cakes as well as a full restaurant menu. Counter service is provided at the entrance, from where you can head to a big first-floor room with high ceilings, furnished with simple tables and chairs and a few comfy sofas. Alternatively you can opt for the paved, tiered garden. Virtually all the food is made in-house, using eggs from humanely reared chickens, along with a great many organic ingredients. The result is an impressive specials board full of the day's snacks and mains, plus an array of tempting cakes. Jasmine and green teas number among the speciality loose-leaf options, and coffee is served by the cup (they grind their own from three choices of bean).

Just a minute's stroll away is the City Museum & Art Gallery, with free admission. It's open daily (10am–5pm), including bank holidays.

Crooked House Tea Rooms

51 High Street, Windsor, Berkshire
Daily 10am–6pm. Closed Easter Sunday, Christmas Day and Boxing Day

Opposite the Tourist Information centre is the unmistakable Crooked House. Years of expanding and contracting unseasoned oak caused the building to tilt, hence its name and shape. Inside is a cosy beamed room on the ground floor and a straight but narrow

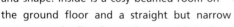

staircase to the first floor, where a table in the window gives a

view of the soldiers marching along the high street during the Changing of the Guard at Windsor Castle. The teashop is renowned for its cream tea (with Cornish clotted cream) and afternoon teas. Gillards of Bath supply the tea, which is loose-leaf. So popular is the Crooked House that queues are likely in the summer, so be prepared to wait.

The Changing of the Guard usually takes place daily April–July (inclusive) and every two days August–March.

Gallery Café & Restaurant

Fisherton Mill, 108 Fisherton Street, Salisbury, Wiltshire
Tues–Sat 10am–5pm. Closed Mon, Sun & bank holidays. Gallery open Mon–Sat 9.30am–5.30pm

Set well back from a city-centre street and occupying a 19th-century grain mill with a tranquil courtyard, the Gallery is a great place to revive yourself. Despite calling itself a café it is included because it supplies speciality teas and because the owner, Michael Fox, produces fabulous food from the best ingredients: cakes, patisseries and puddings are made from double cream, free-range eggs and Belgian chocolate; sandwiches from delicious bread; and vegetarians are

well provided for. The café takes up a significant part of the ground-floor gallery, the first floor housing furniture and fine art, while the second floor has themed art shows.

The courtyard is used as a seasonal space for exhibiting large sculptures and garden pieces – and to enjoy Michael's food alfresco.

The Polly Tea Rooms

26–27 High Street, Marlborough, Wiltshire
Mon–Fri 8.30am–6pm, Sat 8am–7pm, Sun 9am–7pm

This Wiltshire legend has been a tea room for about 100 years and is as popular as ever. You enter the Polly through a patisserie displaying an eye-boggling array of fresh cream gateaux, cakes, and Belgian chocolates. One of the biggest attractions is the cream tea, offering two fresh scones (baked in-house) with either whipped or clotted cream. All the sandwiches,

cakes and gateaux are also prepared on the premises. Vegetarians are well catered for with a great menu that always includes quiche and fish dishes.

The Polly keeps longer opening hours than most

Wiltshire is acknowledged as being the world centre for crop circle sightings. In 2001 a formation appeared at Milk Hill near Alton

teashops in the country and the atmosphere is lively yet relaxed, thanks in part to welcoming and efficient staff. The attractive 400-year-old building, with its beamed ceilings and warm pink walls, is blessed with three distinctive bow windows that look out on to the bustling high street. Chintzy tablecloths give a traditional homely feel but it's far from stuffy, the main room being sizeable, with another room off it. More cream cakes and goodies are displayed in the tea room itself, such as truffles of chocolate, marzipan and pistachio (wrapped in bright green marzipan), among a multitude of others. Green and organic tea number among the speciality options, the coffee is good and home-made lemonade is also available. Children are catered for with their own menu and highchairs are provided.

Polly's has its own shop, which is well worth a visit as you leave. You can buy an entire gateau to take away, or show restraint by opting for one of their own home-made jams or marmalades.

Barnes, measuring nearly 900ft (274m) in diameter and consisting of over 400 separate circles. It was nicknamed 'The Orgasm'.

The Bridge Tearooms

24a Bridge Street, Bradford-on-Avon, Wiltshire
Mon–Sat 9.30am–5pm, Sun 10.30am–5pm

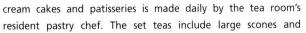

Although the Bridge was originally built as a blacksmith's house in 1675, today the staff wear Victorian-style uniforms. The building has two cosy rooms – one on the ground floor and another on the first, which offers a view of the bridge. A mouth-watering range of gateaux, cream cakes and patisseries is made daily by the tea room's resident pastry chef. The set teas include large scones and

Devonshire clotted cream, while savoury tastes are catered for with rarebits, Wiltshire ham, and muffins. First Flush Darjeeling features among the 17 loose-leaf teas, as do scented exotic teas, and the coffee menu lists 11 types of bean.

A 'broad ford' gave the town its name, serving as a crossing point until the packhorse bridge was built in the 13th century.

Lillie's

High Street, Stockbridge, Hampshire
Daily 8.30am–5pm

Tony Lethbridge gave up a long career as an
architect to pursue his dream of owning a
teashop. He chose this elegant Edwardian-
style establishment in Stockbridge, a popular
but unspoilt little town on the River Test. The
shop is named after Lillie Langtry, a society
hostess and mistress to the Prince of Wales (later Edward VII),
who used to stay in a nearby cottage.

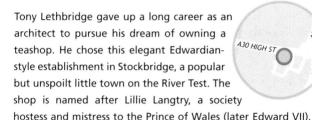

When entering Lillie's you can choose between the
comfortable upholstered seating in the peaceful tea room or
tables on the terrace or in the garden. The food is simple and
good value, the bakery attached producing big scones (the
cream tea is well known, with clotted cream), tasty savoury
pastries and so on, but the generous cakes are home-made
elsewhere specially for them. The teas are loose-leaf and they
have their own blend of coffee, served by the cup or cafetière.

Why not walk off that afternoon tea with a riverside stroll on
Stockbridge Common, accessible from beside the teashop.

Fir Tree House Tea Rooms

Leigh Road, Penshurst, Kent

April–Oct, Tues–Sun 2.30–6pm (closed Mon); Jan–March, weekends only (phone for opening times)

BH

In the heart of a pretty village amid the rolling hills of deepest Kent (near Tunbridge Wells) lies this quintessential tea room. Next door to the village hall, it provides traditional English tea with excellent service in a romantic setting. Fir Tree House has been a

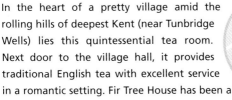

tea room for 70 years and, despite its limited opening hours, deserves inclusion here as a reminder of days gone by. The

eponymous fir tree stood beside the house for 250 years, until it died after a storm.

The unspoilt building is over 400 years old (once a harness-makers, hence the stable doors at the front) and behind it you'll find relaxing, English

Nearby is Penshurst Place, a 650-year-old house and its gardens. The grounds include a plant centre, woodland trail, and adventur

lawned gardens with an abundance of plants and trees. Scent-filled in summer, they are sunny and sheltered, divided into three spaces and furnished with directors' chairs. Inside, the cheerful main room is beamed and tastefully  furnished. A fire burns in the fireplace in winter and another equally atmospheric room is used on busier days.

Caroline Fuller-Rowell has run the tea room since 1985, always being keen to use as many local ingredients as possible. She specializes in creating unusual cakes made to her own recipes, often including fresh, seasonal local fruits. Several cakes, scones and teabreads are freshly made each day, and the teashop also makes its own jam and bread (except that used in the sandwiches, which comprise the only savoury food on the menu). The tea, most of it loose-leaf, is served in distinctive Blue Denmark cups, matching the rest of the crockery, while coffee is served in cafetières.

playground. You can also wander round the toy museum. For further details, call Penshurst Place on 01892 870307.

Claris's

1–3 High Street, Biddenden, Kent
Tues–Sun 10.30am–5.20pm

At one end of a pretty high street and opposite the small village green, lies Claris's, an informal yet traditional teashop in a cosy, white, beamed room dating from 1450 that opens onto a small suntrap of a patio. Brian and Janet Wingham have owned the place since

1984 and ensure that all the food is made in-house, apart from the bread. They excel at huge, melt-in-the-mouth meringues,

served with whipped cream, but there are plenty of cakes, slices or puddings to choose from and a straightforward range of snacks and light meals. A pot of tea goes a long way, thanks to three teabags and a jug of extra water.

Biddenden's oldest house is Vane Court, built around 1420 In 1939 the King of Siam (now Thailand) lived there.

Shepherds Tea Rooms

35 Little London (off East Street), Chichester, West Sussex
Mon–Fri 9.15am–5pm, Sat 9am–5pm

The especially welcoming Shepherds is tucked away just off a main shopping street. The decor is uplifting thanks to fresh green colours and bare wooden floors. Light filters into the main tea room from a conservatory-style room at the back. It's always rewarding

to find loose-leaf teas and the menu offers several, such as Gunpowder or Jasmine. The smooth coffee is sold by the

cup. This teashop makes all its own food, served from breakfast onwards, providing around ten cakes, a roulade of the day and some very popular scones. The house speciality is rarebit (seven to choose from), and cream tea and afternoon tea are offered, both with clotted cream.

Chichester Harbour is an area of outstanding natural beauty, comprising 27 square miles (70sq km) of navigable water.

The Mock Turtle

4 Pool Valley (off East Street), Brighton, East Sussex
Tues–Sat 10am–6pm; sometimes closed for 2 weeks in late spring

  BH

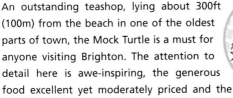

An outstanding teashop, lying about 300ft (100m) from the beach in one of the oldest parts of town, the Mock Turtle is a must for anyone visiting Brighton. The attention to detail here is awe-inspiring, the generous food excellent yet moderately priced and the atmosphere of this 300-year-old building truly memorable. Set on a pedestrianized street, it has a welcoming room on the ground floor, another pretty one downstairs, and several tables outside during the summer months.

Gordon and Birthe Chater have been ensconced here for 30 years, turning the premises into a legend and watching successive generations grow up and bring their own children. All of the food is made in the shop (apart from jams and preserves, which are produced at home), using the finest ingredients and local produce wherever possible. Among the

"If you are cold, tea will warm you; If you are too heated, it will cool you; If you are depressed, it will cheer you; If you are

speciality teas is the delicate and refreshing Lime Blossom, and the Mock Turtle's large teapots (accompanied by extra water) will provide at least three cups.

A great array of cakes is displayed in the window. Two or more fresh cream gateaux are made every day along with baked lemon cheesecake, and the excellent cream teas come with lashings of cream. As you might expect, the tea cakes are big and well spiced and the gingerbread sticky, rich and old-fashioned. All year you can count on a huge variety of big meringues made in different flavours, such as rum and raisin or chocolate, served with local cream. As for savoury dishes, most of the fish is caught locally, the shop is famous for its big, fluffy omelettes, and you can buy snacks such as anchovy toast, which is seldom seen these days. Be prepared to wait for a table during the busiest summer months (July to September).

The Tea Tree

12 High Street, Winchelsea, East Sussex
April–Oct, Mon & Wed–Sun 10am–6pm; Nov–March, Mon & Wed–Sun 10am–5pm. Closed January

The Tea Tree is far bigger than it looks. Four rooms stretch from front to back, each with its own character (one has a wood-burning stove lit in winter), with a small conservatory and garden at the rear. The choice of loose-leaf tea is good and includes Chun Mee Green Tea from China, while the fruit tea is made from dried fruit pieces. The teapots have their own infusers, which you remove

once the tea has brewed to your liking. Coffee is freshly ground from several varieties, including organic. All the food is cooked in-house: choose from several cakes and meringues, five set teas, or the hot dishes and specials.

 Comic legend Spike Milligan used to be a regular at the Tea Tree until his death in 2002. He is buried in the local graveyard.

Pavilion Tea Rooms

Royal Parade, Eastbourne, East Sussex
Oct to mid-May, daily 10am–5pm; mid-May to end Sept, daily 10am–5.30pm

 V   **BH**

Built on the seafront in Edwardian style in 1968, the Pavilion was revamped in 1994. The main space is expansive, decorated with bird of paradise wallpaper, bamboo chairs and marble-topped tables. The staff wear Edwardian-style uniforms, everything is served

in bone china, and a grand piano is played every afternoon in summer (3.30–4.30pm). Teas are loose-leaf (there's also iced tea) and coffees are served in cafetières. All the scones are baked in-house (try the Sussex Cream Tea, with whipped

cream), while sumptuous gateaux and fresh cream pastries are brought in specially. Famed for its breakfast kippers (until 11.30am), the Pavilion offers plenty of other savouries.

Eastbourne's Beachy Head is the highest chalk sea cliff in Britain, rising 530ft (162m) above the sea.

Kandy Tea Room

4 Holland Street (off Kensington Church Street), London W8
Tues–Fri 11am–5pm, Sat & Sun 11am–6pm; closed end of August for a week

The serene and comfortably elegant Kandy Tea Room – named after the owner's Sri Lankan birthplace – is run with outstanding style and attention to detail. All the tea is loose-leaf, from Sri Lanka (previously known as Ceylon), including the excellent Nuwara Eliya, the champagne tea of that country. Tea is served in beautiful Royal Crown Derby bone china accompanied by silver strainers

and cutlery (a real rarity these days), and afternoon tea is presented on silver tiered cake stands. The coffee is supplied by H.R. Higgins of Duke Street and served in cafetières.

The exceptionally friendly and cultured owner, Ananda

The nearest tube is High Street Kensington (three-minute walk); buses along Kensington Church Street are 27, 28, 52, 70 and 328.

Wijesiri, does virtually all the baking himself daily before opening and creates outstanding bread and feather-light scones, using free-range eggs. He also produces excellent light lunches and imaginative sandwiches, while tempting fruit tarts are bought in from the same bakers that supply the House of Commons. The cream tea consists of two scones and clotted cream, served with exceptional jam.

Occupying a mid-19th-century building decorated with William Morris wallpaper in a fruit design, the main tea room is intimate, with classical music playing in the background and the small kitchen visible at the far end. A bigger room downstairs is used chiefly in the winter since the teashop's busiest months are September to June.

On a shelf above the kitchen door you'll see a big cast-iron kettle. This was made in England and belonged to Ananda's mother who kept it over her slow-burning fire at home in Kandy at all times from 1933 to 1979, ready to make tea.

Actress Kate Winslet, Oscar-winning British director Sam Mendes, and comedian Dawn French have all been served here.

The Original Maids of Honour

288 Kew Road, Kew Gardens, Richmond, Surrey
Mon 9.30am–1pm, Tues–Sat 9.30am–6pm

This teashop is bang opposite Kew Gardens, a third of a mile (0.5km) from the Victoria Gate entrance. It has a long history in the same family of bakers of which the current owner, John Newens, is fifth generation.

As you enter the premises you're welcomed by the sight of two counters filled with tempting treats:

patisseries and cream cakes in one, savoury pastries and deep meat or fish pies in the other. All the food is home-made, and the teashop is famous for its Maid of Honour cakes – dainty puff pastries with a sweet

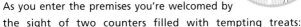

Kew is situated on the south bank of the Thames near Richmond, 6 miles (10km) south-west of central London. The teashop is a five-

curd in their centre, which is served warm. Legend has it that the recipe for the cakes was locked away in an iron chest until rediscovered by King Henry VIII, who presented it to his wife's attendant. With her own hands she made the delicacy, which so pleased the King that he named the cakes Maids of Honour as a compliment to the cook. By the early 18th century, however, a local bakery had been given the recipe and the pastries were enjoyed by fashionable Richmond society. The cakes are still baked using traditional methods and the Newens continue to keep the recipe secret. The building housing the teashop dates back to around 1820, but the shopfront was rebuilt in mock-Tudor style after war damage. There's outdoor seating on a pleasant terrace alongside the building. Inside it's a mellow and slightly sedate affair, with dark wooden tables and bentwood chairs, fresh

flowers on the tables, a carpeted floor, and blue-and-white Spode tableware. Prices are kept low, and so popular is this place that it's advisable to book for lunch all year round (12.30–1.30pm); afternoon teas are served from 2.30pm.

minute walk from Kew Gardens tube station. Buses along Kew Road are the 65 and 391. Victoria Gate is the main entrance to Kew Gardens.

Tea Clipper

53a The Street, Milton Abbas, Dorset

Easter–end Oct, Wed–Sun 10.30am–5.30pm. Closed Mon & Tues and the rest of the year

Milton Abbas is one of the most stunning and peaceful villages in England, with a ribbon of identical 18th-century foursquare cottages of cob and thatch running along a single main street in a deep valley. Since 1990, Pauline and Michael Northeast have run this teashop in one such cottage (well, two knocked into one), with white walls, beamed ceilings and two bay windows.

The Dorset cream tea consists of warm home-made scones accompanied by clotted cream and jam, and the cakes on display (baked by Michael) often include Dorset apple cake served warm with clotted cream. A blackboard menu lists light lunches and a small set menu offers sandwiches and snacks.

The Tea Clipper is only half a mile from the famous 15th-century Milton Abbey in Blandford Forum (open daily from 10am–5.30pm).

The Old Tea House

44 High West Street, Dorchester, Dorset
May–end Oct, Tues–Sun 10am–4.30pm; Nov–end April, Wed–Sun 10am–4pm; closed January

Dating from 1635, the Old Tea House was built as an abbot's house. It stands on one of Dorchester's main streets yet has a tranquil atmosphere, consisting of two rooms (one at the front, with an inglenook fireplace, and another at the back) and a pretty walled garden at the rear. The bay window was added during Victorian times. A tea room for 100 years, it has been run since 1995 by the very friendly Jim and Jan Davie, providing inexpensive traditional English fare. A simple menu offers

snacks and light meals (including rarebits), while home-made warm scones are served for cream tea, and the cakes on show are all made in-house, often featuring Dorset apple cake and Luscious Lemon.

A market is held in Dorchester town centre every Wednesday (8am–3pm) and on Sunday (8am–1pm).

Georgian Tea Room

53 Broad Street, Lyme Regis, Dorset

Daily 10am–5pm (open until later in summer)

BH

Jane Austen may have taken tea in the Georgian Tea Room, when it was a family house, on her visits to Lyme Regis during the early 19th century. Back then this was a thriving trading port. This popular teashop is located on the main street about 300ft (100m) from the sea. At the entrance is a sweet shop, the main tea room being in the unspoilt old kitchen behind it, and at the rear you'll find a delightful enclosed garden. All the tea on the menu is loose-leaf, served in bone china, and coffee is bought by the cup or cafetière. The cakes are all home-made specially for the teashop, often including rich Dorset fruitcake and the equally appetizing Dorset apple cake. The scones come from the local baker and are served warm, while set teas include Jane Austen's Genteel Tea (a cucumber sandwich and cake with tea). Desserts of the day are listed on a blackboard.

Lyme Regis lies within a stretch of coastline awarded World Heritage status because of its superb geology and extensive fossils.

The Colonial Tea House

Abbotsbury Subtropical Gardens, Beach Road, Abbotsbury, Dorset
April–Sept, daily 10am–5.30pm; Oct–March, daily 10am–3.30pm

Nine miles (14km) north-west of Weymouth are Abbotsbury Subtropical Gardens. Set beside the 20-acre (8ha) grounds is the pavilion-style teashop, from which you can sit and listen to the call of the Kookaburra. You order your food at the counter – the ready-wrapped slices of cake are home-made elsewhere. Choices include Yorkshire parkin and orange and lemon Madeira cake. A Dorset cream tea consists of two big scones (ask for them warmed) and a helping of clotted cream, or there's the Dorset apple cake cream tea. Light lunches, and well priced, traditional meals such as steak and kidney pie are offered. Children have their own menu.

Along with the Crown and two London livery companies, the Ilchester family of Abbotsbury are the only people still allowed to own swans.

The Gallery Café

The Devon Guild of Craftsmen, Riverside Mill, Bovey Tracey, Devon

Daily 10am–5pm (Riverside Mill open till 5.30pm)

 V **BH**

In this small historic town on the fringes of Dartmoor lies the attractive Riverside Mill. Built from local stone in 1854 and today home to the Devon Guild of Craftsmen, this is the southwest's leading showcase for top-quality crafts. What's more, admission is free to all events and exhibitions.

Despite its name, the building has never functioned as a mill, but was constructed as a stabling block and outhouses. The water wheel pumped water from the river to supply the horses and the original owner's home. The main gallery upstairs shows seven major exhibitions annually and the ground-floor showrooms display all

Four miles (6.5km) west of Bovey Tracey is Becky Falls Woodland Park, an area of outstanding natural beauty that has been designated a Sit

manner of work. A gift shop sells gifts, cards and books.

The modestly sized Gallery Café backs onto the river and is extremely popular, owing to its excellent food and good value. Approached through a plant-filled courtyard, it manages to be both busy and tranquil, with light from its riverside window reflected off whitewashed stone walls. The sunny courtyard is also furnished with bench tables.

Among the six speciality teas is a decaffeinated option, along with plenty of fruit/herbal choices, and good quality coffee and hot chocolate are served. You can choose from around ten desserts and cakes daily, such as Dorset apple cake and an ample Devon cream tea. A blackboard menu lists a small yet impressive range of savoury dishes (including organic options and a wheat-free dish), plus salads and light meals such as frittata or vegetable tart. The cheese and chive scones are a big hit, served on their own or with fresh soup.

of Special Scientific Interest. Waterfalls and massive boulders form a beautiful rugged landscape, providing a haven for wild animals.

Greys Dining Room

96 High Street, Totnes, Devon
Mon, Tues & Thurs 10am–5pm, Fri 9.30am–5pm, Sat 10am–5pm

A striking array of cakes greets you in the window of this outstanding teashop. Inside, customers are served by staff in traditional black-and-white uniform, and tea is brought to the table on gleaming silver trays. Each day you can choose from around 20 cakes and desserts, all made here and portioned into hefty slices. Devonshire cream tea is served on an elegant glass cake stand and consists of two scones, jams, clotted cream and a pot of tea.

A range of 23 loose-leaf teas includes Indian Prince, Keemun (China), and the list of herbal and fruit infusions will suit any taste. Coffee choices are either filter or decaffeinated.

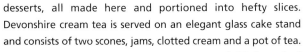

The Norman Totnes Castle commands views over the town and Rive Dart, and is a superb example of motte and bailey construction.

Southern Cross Tearoom & Gardens

High Street, Newton Poppleford, Devon

May, June & Sept, Mon & Wed–Sun midday–5.30pm; July & Aug, daily. Hours vary with seasons

World famous for its cream teas in a stunning setting, Southern Cross is a place of pilgrimage for those bent on witnessing mounds of clotted cream that defy belief. Each day the owners Robin and Kate combine their culinary expertise, with Robin making the excellent scones and all the savouries while Kate creates the cakes and puddings. Local produce is used wherever possible, such as the strawberry jam that accompanies the

clotted cream, which in turn is provided by a pedigree herd of Guernseys (takeaway tubs of cream are for sale). The cream tea consists of two excellent scones, jam, a pot of tea and, of course, a mountain of clotted cream.

Newton Poppleford is part of an area of Outstanding Natural Beauty and lies five miles (8km) from the East Devon Heritage Coast.

Markers Edwardian Restaurant & Delicatessen

High Street, Budleigh Salterton, Devon
Mon–Sat 9am–5.30pm, Sun 11am–5.30pm

The epitome of Edwardian elegance, Markers was built as a tea room in this friendly seaside town in 1910, and the deli (through which you access it) in 1906. After years of neglect the building was bought in 2000 by Nina and Alan Gooch, who have lovingly restored it and attracted a loyal clientele of all ages.

The deli is a treat in itself, the walls and ceiling covered in

the original, honey coloured pitch pine panelling. Here you can buy excellent pies, pasties and other goodies, all made on the premises, alongside other good quality foodstuffs made elsewhere.

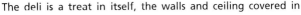

Budleigh Salterton offers unrivalled views of the dramatic gloriou East Devon coastline, officially ranked alongside the Great Barrie

54

You pass through into a grand well-lit space overlooking the high street. Decorated with rich colours, parlour palms, parquet flooring, and walls half-panelled in oak, it has a calm ambience. You are served by extremely friendly and efficient staff who wear traditional black-and-white uniforms. The food is excellent and you can choose from the deli (the almond slices, for example, are very popular) or the tea room menu, which covers everything from morning tea or coffee and snacks, such as locally produced honey-roast ham and great sandwiches, to sophisticated full meals and afternoon teas. In summer they reopen for supper from 7pm. An Edwardian buffet displays a generous range of cakes

and slices, all made on the premises. The full Devon cream tea (with clotted cream, of course) offers two scones and, be warned, they are big. Coffee is served in a cup, mug or cafetière and hot chocolate is also on offer.

Reef as one of the natural wonders of the world. The coast stretches from nearby Exmouth to Old Harry Rocks in Dorset.

55

Georgian Tearoom

Broadway House, 35 High Street, Topsham, Devon

April–Oct, Mon–Tues & Thurs–Sun 8am–4.45pm; Nov–March, same days 8am–4.15pm

The pretty port of Topsham is home to the Georgian Tearoom, within a Grade II* listed house dating from 1777. The single, well-proportioned room benefits from two sash windows looking on to part of the sheltered garden, which has extra seating.

All the food is prepared in-house, using plenty of local produce, and the owner, Heather Knee, makes the jams and most of the cakes – a favourite being

the big scones baked to a traditional recipe. The simple yet homely food is served from breakfast onwards, with roast lunches offered on Tuesday, Thursday and Sunday. The full cream tea is served with clotted cream, and cups of coffee are refilled for free.

The Georgian Tearoom was Devon winner of the Southwest Food and Tourism Award in 2001 and 2002.

Strand Tea Rooms

24 New Street, Barbican, Plymouth, Devon
Mon–Fri 10am–5pm, Sat & Sun 10am–5.30pm

In 1991 Ann Meeson started this popular friendly shop inside an Elizabethan house in the old pedestrianized part of town on a cobbled harbourside quay. There are three rooms (two on the ground floor and one upstairs), and families are welcome. The characterful front room is cosy and light, with a beamed ceiling, portraits of the Tudors hung on a stone wall, and windows giving onto the quay.

Several cakes are displayed in the window, along with fruit pies and slices, and cheesecakes are kept in a chill cabinet. The excellent cream tea offers two warmed, feather-light scones dusted with icing sugar, accompanied by clotted cream and strawberry jam. Coffee is served by the cup or cafetière; a good selection of teas can be purchased, and snacks and meals are available from breakfast onwards.

"Lovely Rita meter maid/May I inquire discreetly/When are you free/To take some tea with me?" From *Lovely Rita*, The Beatles, 1967

The Gateway Tearooms

17 The Square, Moretonhampstead, Devon
Mon & Tues, Thurs–Sun 11am–6pm

At the gateway to the High Moor you'll find a small, relaxed teashop in a merchant's town house of 1491, with bare beams and white walls. It has been a tea room since 1920 and run by Lesley Finch and Ken Brenchley since 1998. Most of the food is made in-house and served in generous portions at good value. Lesley makes around eight cakes daily, along with the plain scones (other scones are frozen) and meringues, all served with

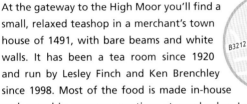

clotted cream from a local farm. The traditional Devonshire cream tea is excellent, coffee is served in a 'bottomless cup', and local organic fruit juices are also on offer. A simple savoury menu includes soups and omelettes, among other light meals.

The Gateway Tearooms has been commended by the *Financial Times* for being 'outstanding in its use of local produce'.

The Corn Dolly

115a East Street, South Molton, Devon
Mon–Sat 9.30am–5pm

The Corn Dolly is best known for its mellow atmosphere, good prices and fabulous food. Everything is made in-house – take your pick from an abundance of huge sponges, deep treacle tarts and so on, displayed on a sideboard and served in huge slices, or try the big teacakes. Other specialities are the Seafarers Tea (locally smoked mackerel fillets with toast and gooseberry sauce) and A King's Ransom (grilled Stilton on a teacake). The list of loose-leaf teas offers unusual choices like Keemun (delicate China

tea) and Rooibos (caffeine-free). The teashop consists of two rooms in a 17th-century listed building (originally stabling for the house next door), which retains much of its original character.

Discover more about the history of the town in the South Molton District Museum, located in The Square.

Primrose Cottage

Lustleigh, near Bovey Tracey, Devon
March–Oct only, Wed–Sun 10.30am–5.30pm

Located next to the village green and originally dating from the 15th century, this thatched cottage painted primrose yellow was rebuilt in 1940. Today it is famous for its cream teas – with two hearty scones, local clotted cream in abundance and two types of jam, strawberry and blackcurrant – and its cakes (loads on view daily). There are also pavlovas, meringues and the hugely

popular lemon and raspberry roulade.

The owner, Caroline Baker, makes all the food in the cottage, including home-made soup of the day, colourful salads and tasty toasties (with a range of toppings, such as salmon and sardine). In fine weather you can sit in the terraced garden overlooking the fast-flowing Wrey Brook.

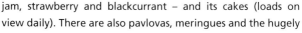

Lustleigh is in Dartmoor National Park. Covering 368 square miles (953sq km), the area is estimated to attract 10 million visitors a year.

Mad Hatter's

28 Church Street, Launceston, Cornwall
June–Oct, Mon–Sat 10am–5pm; Nov–May, Mon–Sat 10.30am–4.30pm

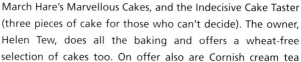

In a hilly northeast Cornwall market town on the River Tamar, this place certainly lives up to its name, with the walls sporting cartoon characters from Lewis Carroll's *Alice in Wonderland*. Tea is served in novelty teapots and the menu is sprinkled with fun titles, like March Hare's Marvellous Cakes, and the Indecisive Cake Taster (three pieces of cake for those who can't decide). The owner, Helen Tew, does all the baking and offers a wheat-free selection of cakes too. On offer also are Cornish cream tea

and the high tea for two; plenty of savoury platters and snacks; coffee by the cup or cafetière; and Chocolate Madness (steaming hot chocolate with whipped cream, marshmallows, and a flake).

Launceston Steam Railway is open to the public until the end of October and takes you on a journey to New Mills.

Rectory Farm

Crosstown, near Morwenstow and Bude, Cornwall

Easter–Oct only, daily 11am–5pm, but best to phone ahead, especially in bad weather

Despite the fact that Rectory Farm is open for only seven months of the year, it is included in this guide because of its location (at the start of a short walk to some of the most spectacular coastal scenery in north Cornwall), the extremely atmospheric 13th-century farmhouse and the quality of the food, all of it made in the farmhouse kitchen in the traditional way. It's well off the beaten track, but worth the adventure and was one of the first teashops to be invited to join the Tea Council's Guild.

In early medieval times the farm and the parish church next to it were owned by monks. The current family has lived here for over 50 years farming beef, sheep and arable. As you step through

The nearby Hawker's Hut is a National Trust building named after the Reverend Robert Stephen Hawker (1803–1875).

the large oak door you head straight back in time, thanks to ancient flagstone floors (that keep it refreshingly cool in summer), heavy oak beams overhead, which were originally taken from wrecked ships, and huge open fireplaces in the two beautifully decorated rooms.

Among the generous selection of teas is the rose-scented Rose Pouchong as well as Smugglers – a blend of Assam, Kenya and Ceylon. The menu offers a modest range of straightforward cooked meals, daily specials and snacks that feature Cornish pasties and local cheeses. Vegetarians have several options. The chutneys and jams are also made here. The Cornish cream tea gives you two big freshly baked scones with clotted cream and all the trimmings, while several hearty cakes are displayed every day, such as the chocolate fudge cake or apple and cinnamon.

When you've finished an afternoon's feasting at the Rectory you can follow a popular 15-minute walk to the tiny and quirky Hawker's Hut, tucked into a cliff with dramatic views.

The eccentric vicar would descend the treacherous cliffs to retrieve the bodies of drowned mariners and give them a Christian burial.

Trenance Cottage Tea Room & Gardens

Trenance Lane, Newquay, Cornwall
March–Oct, daily 10.30am–5pm; phone for winter opening hours; closed November

It is hardly surprising that Trenance Cottage won the Tea Council's Top Tea Place of the Year award in both 2001 and 2002. In addition to its harmonious setting – a Georgian villa of local stone overlooking the attractive public park and lake of Trenance Gardens, and complemented by the tea room's own three-tiered gardens – the service and food are outstanding.

A392 · TRENANCE LN

Judy and Bob Poole have tastefully furnished the small yet elegant tea room with fine antiques, a testimony to Judy's past life as an antiques dealer. (The walnut grandfather clock matches the period of the house.) White linen covers the tables and a bay window faces

"Trenance Cottage Tea Room is setting the standard for top tea making in the UK. Competition for Top Tea Place in 2002 was

one of the garden's two terraces (suntraps sheltered by shrub hedges and small herb gardens), while tables on a lawned section provide views of the tree-lined lake. Virtually all the ingredients used here are sourced locally and all the cakes are made on the premises, using

organic eggs. There are usually five types on offer – displayed on a dresser inside – plus flapjacks, meringues with clotted cream, apple strudel and scones for cream tea. A favourite is the hot ginger parkin served with clotted cream, and the lemon cake gets its mouthwateringly rich yellow colour from the eggs alone. Tea is served in Chatsford teapots, complete with their own strainers inside.

An excellent range of savouries includes fresh local crab, honey-glazed ham, Westcountry cheese with home-made chutney and, of course, great Cornish pasties. For vegetarians, a fresh vegetable soup is always on offer and the Welsh rarebit is popular, as well as the cheese and onion pasties.

ough but Trenance shone through with their exceptionally high standard of service." Bill Gorman, Executive Director for the Tea Council

Bumbles Tea Room

Digey Square, St Ives, Cornwall
June–Oct, Mon–Sat 10am–5pm; Nov–May, Mon–Sat 10am–4.30pm

Renowned all over the world (as testified by a framed copy of an article from *Le Figaro* gracing one wall), Bumbles has a great location – a mere stone's throw from a stunning golden sandy beach in one of the most beautiful and quirky of English towns. It

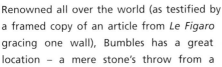

is also just around the corner from Tate St Ives art gallery.
Bumbles may be a small corner tea room in a cottage of at

least 100 years of age, but it is airy and cheerful, thanks partly to its big windows and modern interior of white walls. The main reason, though, is the warmheartedness of the two women who run it, Ann Prisk and Barbara Plummer, who

Tate St Ives opened in June 1993 and offers a unique introduction to modern art, where many works can be viewed in the surroundings

were employed here for years before taking on the business around six years ago. They keep their prices reasonable and make time for people, welcoming families. No wonder their customers keep coming back, year after year.

Apart from their house tea you can choose from five speciality teas, served with an extra jug of hot water and drunk in cups of pretty English porcelain. Coffee-drinkers are served with Cornish coffee. Take your pick from around seven cakes and pastries, all made exclusively for the tea room and brought to the table generously sliced. The Cornish cream tea offers two home-made scones, strawberry jam, Cornish clotted cream and a pot of tea or coffee. Cornish ice cream is also on the menu, served in sundaes and milkshakes, while savouries are limited to simple snacks and salads.

nd atmosphere that inspired them. You'll find the gallery right on he seafront, set in a magnificent location on Porthmeor Beach.

De Wynn's Coffee House

55 Church Street, Falmouth, Cornwall
Mon–Sat 10am–5pm, Sun 11am–4pm

When Falmouth was a busy port in the late 18th century, a Dutch entrepreneur opened De Wynn's as part of a hotel. The fine Georgian building stands in the town centre. The long main room stretches back to a small window with a glimpse of the harbour, and a dumbwaiter delivers the food from the kitchen upstairs.

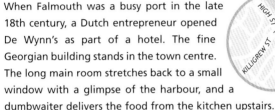

The modest range of speciality teas includes green tea and the shop roasts and grinds its own coffee (8 varieties). A

comprehensive menu boasts delicious Cornish crab for most of the year. The generous cream tea includes Cornish clotted cream, and a dresser shows off the cakes and pastries, most of which are made here.

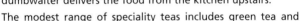

Falmouth is home to the National Maritime Museum Cornwall, which celebrates the history and significance of boats in people's lives.

Auntie's Tea Shop

1 St Mary's Passage (opposite St Mary the Great Church), Cambridge, Cambridgeshire
Mon–Fri 9.30am–6pm, Sat 9.30am–6.30pm, Sun 11am–5.30pm

Housed in a 15th-century building around the corner from Market Square (market every Mon–Sat), the extremely popular Auntie's has been run for over 20 years by Yvonne Prevett. The teashop's big windows look directly on to the grand university church.

Yvonne's staff are particularly courteous and eager to please, decked out in their traditional black-and-white uniforms. The broad and varied menu offers full English breakfasts, light lunches and Auntie's Special Cream Tea, consisting of an egg-and-cress sandwich, two of Auntie's famous scones with jam and cream, and a pot of English breakfast tea. Other favourites are freshly made éclairs dripping with hot chocolate sauce, and the hot banana cake. Five speciality teabag teas are available, plus a decaffeinated version and iced tea. Freshly ground coffee is served by the pot (or iced).

With the Arts Theatre nearby, many actors drop in for tea, including Joanna Lumley, Tony Slattery, Tom Conti and Maureen Lipman.

The Little Tea Room

1 All Saints Passage (off Trinity Street), Cambridge, Cambridgeshire
Mon–Sat 10am–5.30pm, Sun 11am–5.30pm

 BH

Opposite St John's College and overlooking the attractive All Saints Garden, this traditional and homely teashop offers an intimate room on the ground floor, two bigger rooms upstairs (one with sofas), and a small suntrap of a courtyard. Huge Victorian fireplaces and attractive wooden dressers flank you as you eat and drink from pretty blue and white china.

The Little Tea Room is managed by Denise and Glen Ewing, who believe customer care is paramount. They offer a generous choice of loose-leaf teas, such as Gunpowder Green, Keemun (velvet smooth) and China Oolong, and organic teabag Earl Grey and English Breakfast, as well as a small range of coffees. Food begins with all-day breakfasts and light lunches, running through to traditional cream tea (served with clotted cream), Belgian waffles, and an ample range of cakes.

The city is renowned for its bookstores, including the Cambridge University Press, which has sold books since the 16th century.

Connie's Traditional Tea Rooms

4 The Quay, St Ives, Cambridgeshire
Mon–Fri 9.30am–4.30pm, Sat 9.30am–5pm, Sun 10.30am–4.30pm

Connie Stevens turned her back on the City to run her own tea room in this pretty little riverside town. The building overlooks the river and has four comfy rooms – two up, two down – with one set aside for smokers. The food is stunning, ranging from full breakfasts and light lunches with a separate children's menu to a generous variety of tea options, such as cream tea and

Connie's high tea. Also served are great muffins with imaginative fillings and the cakes, desserts and gateaux change daily, among them sumptuous roulades and cheesecakes. The loose-leaf teas include Ceylon and Jasmine, and the coffee and hot chocolate choices are also excellent.

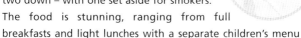

Connie won the 1994 regional finals of the BBC's *Masterchef*, with Loyd Grossman proclaiming her Masterchef of the East of England.

The Orchard

45–47 Mill Way, Grantchester, Cambridge

Daily 10am–7pm (but can vary according to season and events, so phone ahead)

 V   BH ♇

For a quintessentially English tea experience you can't beat the Orchard at Grantchester, a genteel setting enjoyed by generations of Cambridge students and visitors from all over the world. The orchard from which the teashop takes its name is over 100 years old and the best time to see it is when it is in bloom (late spring and early summer). Here it feels as though time stands still, and you

can take advantage of the deckchairs under the trees and soak up the sunshine; on cooler days there's the option of the atmospheric enclosed pavilion, which overlooks the grounds and is heated in the winter.

The on-site Rupert Brooke Museum (free, open daily 10am–4pm) tells the story of the poet who, before his death at the age of 27,

The story of the Orchard began in 1897, when a group of students were served tea under the blossoming fruit trees rather than on the front lawn of Orchard House, which had been the custom. Little did they know that they had started what was to become a great Cambridge tradition. In 1909 a young poet called Rupert Brooke lodged at Orchard House and fell in love with the idyllic way of life while at the same time forging friendships with the likes of Virginia Woolf and E.M. Forster. Later, in a homesick mood on a trip to Berlin, Brooke wrote his most famous poem *The Old Vicarage, Grantchester*, a framed copy of which is in the pavilion.

You place your food orders in the servery before continuing on to either the orchard or pavilion. All the good-value eats are made on-site, including great scones (served with Cornish clotted cream), fresh cream cakes and gateaux, several savoury dishes and daily specials (usually a vegetarian option). In winter a roast beef lunch is made every day.

Today the orchard has been left, where possible, to grow semi-wild and unkempt, as it was in the past. On summer evenings, however, a new tradition of outdoor performances of Shakespeare, Mozart and other productions have become part of the Cambridge Fringe Festival.

was inspired to write the most famous of tea-related lines: 'Stands the church clock at ten-to-three/And is there honey still for tea?'

Sally Lunn's

4 North Parade Passage, Bath, Somerset
Mon–Sat 10am–6pm, Sun 11am–6pm

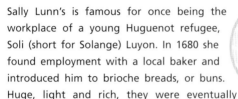

Sally Lunn's is famous for once being the workplace of a young Huguenot refugee, Soli (short for Solange) Luyon. In 1680 she found employment with a local baker and introduced him to brioche breads, or buns. Huge, light and rich, they were eventually served at the public breakfasts and afternoon teas that were

so popular in Georgian Bath, and could be enjoyed with sweet or savoury accompaniments. Over time the bread came to be known as the Sally Lunn Bun. This elegant teashop, which dates back to around 1482, occupies three stories, each room tastefully decorated with period pieces. The Sally Lunn Bun is still baked by hand to the original secret

In the building's cellars is a small museum (with free admission for teashop customers), revealing the Roman and medieval

recipe. The best way to eat it is cut in half and toasted, smothered in savoury or sweet toppings. The menu presents you with all manner of choices, such as a Welsh rarebit creation, jam and clotted cream (pictured right), or Scottish smoked salmon and fresh lemon juice. The house  speciality is one of the several cream teas, such as the Bath cream tea, served with a topping of cinnamon butter and a mound of local clotted cream.

If you're after something a little more substantial then you can't go far wrong by ordering a Trencher. Traditionally a type of bread, a Trencher is effectively an edible plate that you consume as you devour its contents – Westcountry beef in red wine, or mushroom stroganoff, for example.

Sally Lunn's teas are loose-leaf, among them a fruit tisane, and the freshly roasted coffee is bought by the cup or cafetière from a list of several speciality blends.

The teashop can get exceptionally busy so be prepared to queue at lunchtimes between June and September.

foundations of the house, excavation finds, as well as the original bakery kitchen with the faggot oven used by Sally Lunn herself.

Bilbys Coffee Shop

Market Street, Crewkerne, Somerset
Mon–Fri 9am–5pm, Sat 9am–5pm

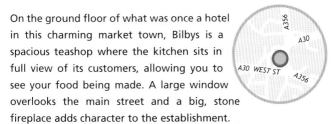

On the ground floor of what was once a hotel in this charming market town, Bilbys is a spacious teashop where the kitchen sits in full view of its customers, allowing you to see your food being made. A large window overlooks the main street and a big, stone fireplace adds character to the establishment.

The owners, Jane and Tris Pinkney, use mostly local ingredients and provide a huge range of cakes, roulades and desserts, all on display. The delicious Somerset apple cake is served warm (clotted cream optional). Most of the menu food is made by Bilbys Traditional Foods of Yeovil and offers potted Somerset smokies (made with local smoked fish) in an otherwise simple selection of full and light meals. A board advertises all-day breakfasts and daily specials. Newspapers and magazines are supplied, and a family table is tucked away.

Wednesday is market day in Crewkerne, and a farmers' market is usually held on the last Saturday of the month.

Vellow Tea Gardens

Vellow, near Williton, Somerset
Easter–late autumn only, daily 2–6pm

Eleven miles (18km) from Dunster Castle lies the tiny village of Vellow. Set in the village centre, the tea gardens occupy an acre (0.5ha) of ground and were created from scratch 30 years ago. Today you can enjoy lush lawns, mature trees and a stream. An attractive outdoor terrace provides most of the seating. All the food is made in-house from local ingredients, such as

free-range eggs. The big cheese and herb scones are popular, as is the full cream tea (all scones are served warm). There are also fine selections of cakes, desserts and savouries. The choice of speciality teas varies.

"Love and scandal are the best sweeteners of tea."
Henry Fielding (1707–54), *Love in Several Masques* (1728)

Lewis's Tea Rooms

13 High Street, Dulverton, Somerset
Daily 10am–5pm; closed one week in January

 BH

An especially friendly and relaxing teashop is Lewis's. Two knocked together 18th-century cottages form a spacious room with yellow walls and a stone fireplace at either end (they burn in winter). Kathie and David Fuller have run the shop since 2000 and won a Tea Council award two years later. Local ingredients are used where possible and Kathie bakes most of the cakes; big scones are made daily, together with puddings. The menu offerings

begin with breakfast followed by various rarebits, such as the Somerset version (made with cider and topped with Brie), and a choice of four cream teas. The drinking tea is loose-leaf, and coffee is served in a cafetière.

 Dulverton lies between the rivers Barle and Exe, and Exmoor's Winsford Hill moorland is a few miles up the Barle valley.

The Abbey Tea Rooms

16 Magdalene Street, Glastonbury, Somerset

Daily 10am–5pm (till 5.30pm during school holidays)

Opposite the abbey lies this traditional teashop that has been run by Mary Parker since 1989. The tables are dressed in linen and the staff in old-fashioned uniforms. All the food is made in-house, relying chiefly on local ingredients. Among the daily choice of sweets is Cider Cake, served warm with clotted cream, as are the scones in the Somerset cream tea, for which the teashop is renowned. The speciality teas include Jasmine and Rose Pouchong, and a choice of coffees is served by the cup, mug or cafetière. The local cider (Sheppy's Oakwood) is also available, along with lager, wine and sherry.

Rolf Harris has paid a visit to this teashop, and Edward Enfield (Harry's father) was filmed here for one of his TV appearances.

The Black Cat

High Street, Lechlade, Gloucestershire
Generally daily, 9.30am–4.30pm or 5.30pm. NB Phone ahead

This 18th-century building doubles as a modest tea and coffee retailers. Dame Grey is blended in-house and there's a great range of loose-leaf teas, plus several fruit-flavoured ones (China black tea mixed with natural oils, leaves or petals). The coffee is ground on the premises from an excellent range of beans, such as the smooth Guatemala Elephant bean (so-called because it's a third or so larger than other beans). The food is all made

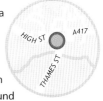

in-house, including cakes and scones with clotted cream for the cream tea, and savoury meals such as all-day breakfasts, several rarebits, daily specials and a children's menu.

The nearby Cotswolds, an area of outstanding natural beauty, is famed for its rolling hills and charming villages.

Thatchers

101 Montpellier Street, Cheltenham, Gloucestershire
Mon 9am–2pm, Tues–Sat 9am–5pm

On a quiet street in the centre of this spa town, the elegant and cheerful Thatchers is run with great flair by Jean-Brice Raybaud. He does most of the cooking, including the full English breakfast, and is visible hard at work in the kitchen. Choose a quick lunch or go for something bigger from the daily specials, such as fillet

of salmon with dill sauce. Among the specialities are great omelettes, delicious tarts and out-of-this-world scones, which are served warm with clotted cream when you order cream tea. The cakes and cheesecakes are made specially for Thatchers. Upstairs is a quieter room that faces the impressive-looking 19th-century Cheltenham Ladies' College.

Charles Dickens was so taken with Cheltenham he once remarked: "Rarely have I seen such a place that so attracted my fancy".

The Antique Teashop

40 High Street, Ross-on-Wye, Herefordshire

Easter–Nov, Mon–Sat 9.45am–5pm, Sun 10.15am–5pm. Hours vary with seasons

Set high on a sandstone cliff, with a commanding view over the River Wye, is the historic market town of Ross-on-Wye. Situated in the heart of rural Herefordshire and in the picturesque Wye Valley the area has become a popular destination for tourists. A fabulous collection of timber houses dating from the Tudor

period is dotted around the 17th-century Market House. These beautiful surroundings provide the perfect setting for the town's markets (held on Thursdays and Saturdays between 9am and 3.30pm), which offer a wide

The Ross-on-Wye International Festival first took place in August 200 on the banks of the River Wye. The event featured world-famou

82

selection of goods including jewellery, watercolours, fresh produce, books and pot plants.

Entering the teashop is like stepping into a comfy Georgian drawing room, and then you discover that all the antiques you see on display are for sale. This includes the bone china tableware and even the armchairs and settees you sit on.

The exceedingly welcoming Mrs Cockin runs this establishment, the sister shop to another of the same name in Hereford (*see* overleaf). Her daughter Jane owns both and trained at the Savoy. The huge scones are legendary, made (like the cakes) by the local baker. All the other food is made in the teashop. The teas are loose-leaf, the menu comprehensive and the prices reasonable. Take your pick between the traditional cream tea and a bigger afternoon tea.

tists such as Van Morrison, Atomic Kitten, Lulu, Alistair McGowan nd Harry Hill. The festival is set to become an annual occasion.

The Antique Tea Shop

5a St Peter's Street, Hereford, Herefordshire
Mon–Sat 9.45am–5pm, Sun 10.15am–5pm

Operated along the same lines as its sister teashop in Ross-on-Wye (*see* previous pages), this is also owned by Jane Cockin, who came up with the idea of running a teashop-cum-antiques shop with a difference. Everything you see before you is for sale; all the furniture, mirrors and so on that complete the feel of a Georgian

drawing room that is elegant yet slightly eccentric. Jane ensures there are always a couple of Regency-style sofas. Try the huge scones and the lightest of cakes, all made specially for the teashop. Other attractions are the loose-leaf tea, the traditional cream tea with clotted cream and the bigger afternoon tea.

Housed within Hereford Cathedral is the *Mappa Mundi*, the mos elaborate, complete, pre-15th-century world map in existence.

Harriet's

20 High Street, Woodstock, Oxfordshire
Mon–Fri 8.30am–5pm, Sat 8.30am–5.30pm, Sun 10am–5.30pm

The pretty Cotswold town of Woodstock is home to Harriet's, a cake shop and patisserie with a teashop attached. Owned by Judi and Paul Parker-Jones, the building dates from 1627 and contains two beamed tea rooms with bare stone walls. Dogs are allowed in the attractive paved garden. All the soups and savouries are made in the kitchen (the soups are generous and free of meat stock) to include daily specials. The cakes, gateaux and scones are all locally home-made and the local baker provides the

fresh bread, pies and French-style patisseries. The cream tea offers Cotswold clotted cream and the day's meals begin with breakfast. Choose from four types of coffee, available by cup or cafetière.

Woodstock is perhaps best known for Blenheim Palace, home of the 11th Duke of Marlborough and birthplace of Sir Winston Churchill.

Haskett's

86b South Street, Dorking, Surrey
Mon–Sat 9am–5pm, Sun 11am–5pm

Central Dorking is home to Haskett's, where you'll find outstanding traditional food at great value in a 17th-century Grade II listed building. It comprises a main room on the ground floor with an open kitchen at the end and a small quiet room downstairs. The house tea is Broken Orange Pekoe while other loose-leaf teas include four Premium Estate teas, such as the extremely rare

Mountains of the Moon, and 16 other speciality ones, like Matte (Argentina's national drink as well as being Brazil's favourite tea). Coffee is made from a choice of pure arabica beans. Food-wise there's a good range of breakfasts, plus daily hot specials such as rarebits, corned beef hash and eggs benedict.

Sir Laurence Olivier, considered one of history's greatest actors, was born in Dorking. He died in 1989 at the age of 82.

Benson's

4 Bards Walk (off Henley Street), Stratford-upon-Avon, Warwickshire
Mon–Sat 8.30am–5.15pm, and Sunday during June–Sept and Nov–Dec, 11am–4.30pm

A short walk from William Shakespeare's birthplace lies this contemporary venue – not what you would expect from a town steeped in history. The intimate split-level room has a Continental feel – granite-topped tables, upholstered chairs and, best of all, patisseries delivered fresh every morning from Maison Blanc (run by Raymond Blanc). Feast your eyes on supplies of tarte au citron, millefeuille, éclairs and more, the range varying from day to day. Presentation and efficiency are also impressive. Both the full afternoon tea and champagne tea are delivered on tiered cake stands. A full range of high quality food is served from breakfast onwards and Benson's is well known for gourmet sandwiches. Taylor's of Harrogate supply the loose-leaf tea and the coffee, the latter offered by cup or cafetière. Bookings are recommended for lunch and afternoon tea.

No trip to Stratford-upon-Avon is complete without paying a visit to Shakespeare's birthplace, a half-timbered house in Henley Street.

"Tea is drunk to forget the din of the world."

T'ien Yiheng, Chinese sage

Northern England

The Chantry Tearooms

9 Chantry Place, Morpeth, Northumberland
Mon–Sat 9am–4.45pm

Opposite the Tourist Information centre (which is housed in the restored Morpeth Chantry) sits this small, traditional and long-established teashop, run by Frances Johnson. It's a cheery room, with bench seating in the window. A pine dresser shows off the day's cakes – usually eight or so – and all the food is made on the premises. The speciality teas are loose-leaf and the coffee

choices adequate, while local ginger beer, lemonade and mineral water are also available. The menu runs from breakfast through to cream tea and the satisfying afternoon tea for two, and there's also a children's menu.

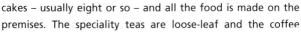

The Morpeth Chantry also houses a bagpipe museum, open Monday to Saturday 10am–5pm. Admission to this unusual museum is free.

The Copper Kettle

21 Front Street, Bamburgh, Northumberland

July & Aug, daily 10.30am–5pm, rest of the year, Tues–Sun 10.30am–5pm. Closed Dec & Jan

In the shadow of Bamburgh Castle, the Copper Kettle inhabits one of six 18th-century cottages. It is decorated with the original hand-carved oak panelling and an assortment of copper kettles hanging from two beams. Pat and Heather Green moved here from Rhodesia, and all the cakes are made to Heather's

Rhodesian recipes, with names like Boston Bread (date loaf) and Luscious Lemon Loaf. The sandwiches are generous and another bonus is the locally caught crab. Some unusual fruit infusions are offered, and three speciality blends of coffee.

Overlooking the North Sea and dominating the Northumbrian landscape, Bamburgh Castle is open from April to October.

The Market Place

29 Market Place, Barnard Castle, County Durham

March–Oct, Mon–Sat 10am–5.30pm, Sun 2.30am–5.30pm; rest of year Mon–Sat 10am–5.30pm

This friendly teashop in the historic market town of Barnard Castle (known locally as 'Barney') has been owned for over three decades by Bob Hilton and Roy Varndell. A hoard of regulars mingles effortlessly with a steady flow of holidaymakers to create a pleasant ambience. Set in an unassuming yet welcoming environment of 18th-century bare stone walls and stone-flagged floors, you can appreciate good food at great prices here. Roy does some of the baking and creates excellent scones, along with Yorkshire curd tart and fruit tarts, to name but a couple. A specials board offers straightforward meals such as home-made steak pie with vegetables at irresistible prices. There's a good range of tea, and coffee is available by the cup or cafetière. The Artisan shop upstairs sells chinaware (such as Spode), glassware, prints and original works of art.

The grounds and ruins of 12th-century Barnard Castle are within easy walking distance of the Market Place.

Farrer's

13 Stricklandgate, Kendal, Cumbria

Mon–Sat 9am–4.45pm

The hugely atmospheric Farrer's is a long-established tea and coffee merchants. The building dates to 1640 when it was a packhorse inn. Enjoy the aroma of fine teas and coffees on your way through to the main teashop – a bustling ground-floor room – or visit the quieter rooms upstairs. Coffee is roasted on the premises and all the food is made in-house. You can enjoy a generous

supply of cakes as well as afternoon tea, three different types of scone, and a good range of savoury dishes. Among the speciality teas are Jasmine and Oolong. Children have their own menu.

Kendal lies just outside the Lake District National Park, about 10 miles (16km) south of Windermere and 5 miles (8km) from Staveley.

Bryson's

38–42 Main Street, Keswick, Cumbria
March–Oct, daily 8.30am–5pm (till 5.30pm July & Aug). Other opening times vary

The northern gateway to the lakes is blessed with an excellent bakery-cum-patisserie in the town centre, with a friendly traditional tea room above it. This is a family business set in relaxing surroundings. The spacious Victorian room has large windows overlooking the street and is simply yet comfortably furnished. The mood is a little sedate, with the teashop's attentive waitresses wearing uniforms, but it's in no way stuffy. Prices are

reasonable and the water in the Lake District makes an especially tasty cuppa. Bryson's policy is to bake as much food as possible every morning, so best arrive early for the widest

Serious climbers will relish nearby Skiddaw (3054ft/931m), Helvellyn (3113ft/949m) and Scafell Pike (3205ft/977m). The inexperienced can

selection. It's all well prepared from the best ingredients and served in generous portions, beginning with breakfast. The biggest seller is the Lakeland Plum Bread (a lightly spiced fruit bread taking its name from the traditional term for dried fruit), which is toasted and buttered. Other specialities are the Finest Fruitcake (rich like a Christmas cake) and substantial afternoon teas served on tiered cake stands. The Lakeland cream tea, for example, offers apple pie, fruitcake, fruit maltloaf and plum bread with your scone, plus several accompaniments such as rum butter. Another big attraction is the supply of melt-in-the-mouth cream cakes, pastries, gateaux and fruit flans, fresh from the bakery, which you

can contemplate from two counters. For those with simpler tastes, scones and teacakes are also on the menu. Hot meals include such offerings as poached local Borrowdale trout, home-roasted ham or beef, and the delicious Cumberland sausages.

lso enjoy splendid views of the surrounding countryside by scaling he smaller Latrigg (1204ft/367m) and Catbells (1500ft/445m).

The Hazelmere Café

1 Yewbarrow Terrace, Grange-over-Sands, Cumbria
Easter to mid-Nov, daily 10am–5pm; rest of the year, daily 10am–4.30pm. Closed Mon in Jan & Feb

 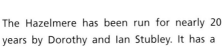

The Hazelmere has been run for nearly 20 years by Dorothy and Ian Stubley. It has a bakery attached and stands in a line of shops under attractive Victorian verandas opposite ornamental gardens with a lake.

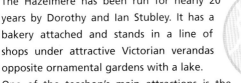

One of the teashop's main attractions is the astounding range of teas, all loose-leaf and single-estate. Many of them are green, several are organic. There are teas

from India, Sri Lanka, Africa, Argentina, China and Japan, each with its own informative tasting notes. You'll find exotic names like Ambootia Estate (Darjeeling), and Mahagastotte Estate, a Sri Lankan champagne of teas.

An unusual health-promoting tea offered here is Yerba Maté (pronounced Ma-tay), brewed from the leaves of a Latin

Guest teas and coffees are also regularly featured. The coffee is good, freshly roasted by Farrer's of Kendal (*see* p.93) and served by the cup or by cafetière.

The ambience is refined yet welcoming, in a big room with a high ceiling and windows along the full length of the facade. Classical music plays in the background as you're served by the efficient staff. The imaginative food is also outstanding and all made on the premises using the best of ingredients like free-range eggs and vegetarian cheese. All sorts of cakes, slices, tarts and desserts are shown off at the counter, such as Cumberland Rum Nicky or Yorkshire Curd Tart. The extensive menu offers plenty of mains (like West Indian lamb with Caribbean rice), light meals and snacks plus several tasty vegetarian options every day. You might find griddled Penrith goats' cheese served with sweet-and-sour cherry tomatoes and salad, along with bread from the bakery. Daily specials are also offered and there's an extensive children's menu.

American holly tree. It is traditionally drunk from a gourd and sipped through *una bombilla* (a metal straw), as supplied at the Hazelmere.

Betty's Café Tea Rooms

6–8 St Helens Square, York, North Yorkshire
Daily 9am–9pm, but Belmont Room only Sat 11am–4pm & Sun midday–2pm

This classic English tea room, one of five of the same name in Yorkshire, opened in 1936 and offers stunning period architecture and a tremendous atmosphere. Such is its popularity that you may well have to queue to get in. Also, be prepared for higher prices than you might expect in other teashops, but remember

you're paying for a special experience and you should enjoy the indulgence! On the first floor is the magnificent Belmont Room – an exact replica of a 1930s stateroom from the liner *Queen Mary* (open only on Sat 11am–4pm and for traditional Sunday lunch midday–2pm). Entirely glass-fronted, the building is filled with light. On the

This teashop is the older sister of Little Betty's, just up the roa (see p.100), and the younger sister of Betty's in Harrogat

ground floor is the main tea room (as pictured). Downstairs, the Oak Room has a quieter mood and a more sedate pace.

Betty's owes its distinction to sheer style and the astonishing attention to detail of a bygone era, such as silver teapots and strainers, a cake-laden trolley brought to your table, and attentive service from staff in black-and-white uniforms. All the food is delivered fresh each morning in 1920s-style vans, the mouthwatering cakes and pastries having been made at their craft bakery in Harrogate. A speciality is the Yorkshire Fat Rascal, a big, plump fruity scone, served warm, but the generous menu offers all sorts of temptations like cream tea, an excellent afternoon tea and an extensive range of savouries. Children are provided with the Little Rascals menu. Apart from the house blend, all the tea is loose-leaf, with a

few interesting options, such as Ceylon Blue Sapphire (with blue flecks of cornflower) and a rare green tea from Taiwan. The coffee list is equally impressive, served by the cup or the cafetière.

see p.101). The other two 'relatives' are Betty's in Ilkley (West Yorkshire) and there's also one in Northallerton (North Yorkshire).

Little Betty's

46 Stonegate, York, North Yorkshire
Daily 9am–5.30pm

The cosiest shop in the Betty's empire (*see previous pages and opposite*), this is two minutes' walk from its big sister, above a tea and coffee outlet in a pedestrianized shopping street in the city centre. You enter a welcoming environment of three knocked-through rooms with cream-coloured walls, marble-topped

tables, and there's another room at the back. All of the Betty's hallmarks are here: great service and attention to detail; mouthwatering cakes and patisseries; sumptuous afternoon tea; and a wealth of savouries to choose from, as long as you don't mind paying extra for the experience. Children are made especially welcome.

 Stonegate is the main shopping street in the York Minster region of the city and is popular with musicians and artists

Betty's Café Tea Rooms

1 Parliament Street, Harrogate, North Yorkshire
Daily 9am–9pm

This is the shop that launched the family-run Betty's empire, although it was originally located across the road where Jaeger stands today. The tea room was established in 1919 by Frederick Belmont, a Swiss confectioner, and it blossomed into five Yorkshire teashops.

At the entrance is a high-quality craft bakery where you can feast your eyes on a multitude of patisseries, fine chocolates and other temptations. It's most likely that you will join a queue to the elegant tea rooms, reached down a short flight of stairs. The first magnificent room looks on to a park and is decorated with parlour palms, marble-topped tables and a grand piano. Downstairs is a wood-panelled room, bearing marquetry pictures by an artist called Charles Spindler and his son, Paul, made in Alsace using inlaid pieces of wood. As in all the Betty's shops, children are warmly welcomed.

The grand piano is played daily 6–9pm and on Sunday 9am–midday, usually classical or music from the 1920s and 30s.

The Lavender Tea Rooms

16 Market Place, Knaresborough, North Yorkshire
Mon–Sat 10am–4.30pm, Sun 11am–4.30pm

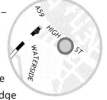

Above the oldest chemist's shop in England – established in 1720 – these tea rooms are named after the lavender water that has been sold from this site for centuries. Today the shop sells fine teas and coffees, chocolate and other confectionery such as Farrah's fudge and toffee (made in Harrogate). Everything else is made on the premises to include a good range of cakes, and lavender is

even used in some of the baking, such as the popular lemon and lavender scones. Several organic teas are available, while some of the other teas are supplied by Farrer's of Kendal (*see p.93*), who also provide the coffee.

"Thank God for tea! What would the world do without tea? How did it exist? I am glad I was not born before tea." Sydney Smith (1771–1845)

Moonraker Floating Tearoom

1 Commercial Mill, Slaithwaite, Huddersfield, West Yorkshire

April–end Sept, Tues–Sat 9am–6pm, Sun 10am–6pm (closed Mon); phone ahead for rest of the year

On a quiet canal in the beautiful Colne Valley is Moonraker – a floating teashop – where walkers, cyclists and tourists are the most frequent customers to this narrow boat. Valerie Todd had the vessel purpose-built and started to serve good-value food in 1992. You can park beside the canal and hop aboard. Easy, shallow steps take you down to the honey-coloured interior, fully

lined with pine boarding. Apart from the ice cream, all the food is made in the galley: hot and cold snacks, scones, cakes and the best-seller almond tarts. Orange Pekoe from Ceylon is on offer and coffee is served by the cup.

Slaithwaite is the setting for much of the filming for the ITV series *Where The Heart Is* – known as Skelthwaite in the programme.

Exchange Coffee Company

13–15 Fleming Square, Blackburn, Lancashire
Mon–Sat 9am–5pm (shop closes 5.30pm)

Despite the proprietor's choice of name for this drinking establishment, Blackburn's Exchange Coffee Company certainly deserves a mention as a teashop. When it comes to tea you're spoilt for choice here since this is primarily a shop selling fine teas and coffees –

over 40 fine varieties of tea (black, green or Oolong), along with 25 or more arabica coffees, freshly roasted on-site and supplied to several businesses around the country. Unusually, the tea is brought to the table in a cafetière, a great idea since it prevents over-brewing. Several varieties of herbal tisanes and fruit infusions are also available.

The Exchange Coffee Company has operated for more than a decade. Inhabiting part of a tastefully refurbished Victorian shopping arcade (one of the few old buildings left in Blackburn) from which it takes its name, the big mellow tea

The Blackburn Museum & Art Gallery, situated in the town centre, opened in 1872, originally as both a museum and a library. Japanese

room is kitted out with William Morris wallpaper, old oak panelling along one wall, an impressive stone fireplace, Georgian settles and antique chairs. It's a place to sit back and relax in the city centre; indeed the menu requests that people switch off their mobile phones.

The clientele consists mainly of locals who enjoy working lunches, and visitors from nearby smaller towns. They come for the delicious food, mostly made in-house, though the generous selection of cakes, desserts and slices is bought in. If you try just one sweet then make it the Chocolate Junkyard, a chocolate pastry filled with a layer of rich ganache piled high

with mousse and heaped with chunks of chocolate. The fruit smoothies are also delicious. As well as snacks there are daily specials listed on a board, and smaller portions are prepared for children on request.

prints, rare books and coins, illuminated manuscripts and religious icons are just some of the highlights housed in the building today.

Exchange Coffee Company

24 Wellgate, Clitheroe, Lancashire
Mon–Sat 9am–4.45pm (shop closes 5.30pm)

Like its sister company in Blackburn (*see previous pages*), this reasonably priced shop deserves a mention because of its huge choice of fine loose-leaf teas, sold in the shop at the front along with an impressive range of freshly roasted coffees. The late 1800s building sits in a quiet street in the middle of town and

has a fairly refined, relaxed feel, renovated in Victorian style. Choose between a cosy tea room on the ground floor and another on the first floor. You'll find a modest selection of specially made sweets – the Dime Bar cake is a must – as well as several daily specials prepared in-house.

Clitheroe is the main market town of the Ribble Valley, the picturesque location where the Queen, it is said, would like to retire.

Tiffins

The Square, Marsh Mill, Thornton, Lancashire
Mon–Fri 10.30am–5pm, Sat 10am–5pm, Sun 11am–5pm

   V

In this small town the intimate and cheery Tiffins sells over 200 varieties of packeted tea and coffee, which is fitting because the word 'tiffin' originated as a colloquialism for tiffing – to take a little drink or sip. Tea room customers can choose from any of the brews and the coffee is freshly ground throughout the day.

The business is run by the ultra-hospitable Stewart and Melody Urwin and is part of a purpose-built 'village' constructed in the late 1980s at the base of a windmill that is now a museum. A menu of excellent food is virtually all made in-house, producing a generous range of gateaux, tarts and puddings. Savoury specialities are Borrowdale tea loaf and Lancashire cheese, big wedges of cheese and onion pie, and Loch Fyne kiln-roast salmon (all year). Organic dishes are offered every other week; and there's also a children's menu.

One of the largest of its kind in Europe, Marsh Mill is open from April to end Oct, daily 10.30am–5pm; rest of year, daily 11am–4pm.

The Coffee Bean

77 Clifton Street, Lytham St Anne's, Lancashire
Mon–Sat 9.30am–5pm, Sun 11.30am–5pm

Despite its name this shop is included because of its wide range of loose-leaf teas (15) and ample selection of cakes and pastries, specially made and usually featuring a fresh-cream gateau. The Coffee Bean also sells a particularly generous cream tea.

Set in a modernized old cottage on Lytham's main shopping street, this simple tea room is reached through a shop selling fine teas and coffees. The menu lists a number of speciality teas from different parts of the world (among them fruit-flavoured China teas) but you can choose from any of the China teas in the shop. Twelve special coffees are listed in the tea room, but again you can pick from any of the beans in the shop to be specially ground for you and then enjoyed by the cafetière or cup. For foodies, the marinated herrings with dill are especially popular, and Lancashire cheese is also sold here.

Lytham and St Annes are in fact two distinct towns; St Annes-on-Sea being a seaside town, while leafy Lytham enjoys a village atmosphere.

Charlotte's

The Square, Great Eccleston, Preston, Lancashire
Mon–Sat 10am–5pm, Sun 11am–5pm

Margaret Cookson opened Charlotte's in the late 1990s and today it is well known for its food and loose-leaf tea. All the food is home-made in her kitchen at home, her brother bakes the cakes, of which there are several on the menu daily, and her husband contributes to the meat and fish dishes such as the smoked mackerel and avocado sandwiches. You can choose from

seven varieties of coffee, served in a cafetière, and the afternoon tea includes great smoked salmon sandwiches. All of the meals are brought to the tables on pretty blue-and-white Spode china tableware.

This rural village in the centre of the Fylde plain was recorded in the Domesday book as Eglestun, meaning 'the place of the church'.

Katie's

38 Watergate Street, Chester, Cheshire
Mon–Sat 10am–5pm, Sun 10am–4pm

Katie's greatest attraction is its stunning location – a Grade II listed building constructed in about 1300 as a merchant's house in the attractive pedestrianized part of central Chester. Hiding behind an imitation 17th-century facade (the gallery above the entrance), it is one of the city's oldest buildings still in use today. The main tea room was originally an undercroft, a big

storage space for goods, and is an impressive affair of bare stone walls, oak trusses, old wooden floors and a window on to the thoroughfare. The first-floor room is simpler, with white stone walls and smaller beams.

Chester's town criers declare midday proclamation every Tuesday to Saturday at the High Cross from May to August – the only place in

Presentation and good-value food are important here. Tea is served in sterling silver teapots and the full afternoon tea is presented on a silver tiered cake stand. Keemun Best (an especially smooth and light China tea) and Rose Petal (a soft, delicate black China tea) feature among the good range of speciality loose-leaf teas.  Coffee connoisseurs can sip the much sought-after Ethiopian Mocha Sidamo or the 'champagne of Kenya', Estate Grown Kenya Peaberry, each served in cafetières, or choose coffee by the cup. Most of the food is baked or prepared on the premises apart from a few of the cakes such as éclairs and vanilla slices, which are home-made locally. The food is traditional, kicking off with the full English breakfast and then later you might want to try Katie's Special: a ham and cheese sandwich coated in breadcrumbs and deep-fried so that the cheese melts. A well-priced two-course lunch is offered from Monday to Friday, and a children's menu operates all week (high chairs are also available).

Britain to boast such regular appearances. Chester's own David and Julie Mitchell are the world's first husband-and-wife crier partnership.

Nostalgia Tea Rooms

219 Lord Street, Southport, Merseyside

July to Sept, Tues–Fri 9.30am–4.30pm, Sat 9.30am–5pm, Sun 10am–5pm. Hours vary with seasons

These tea rooms have been run since 1989 by the gregarious Ann Couzens. A single room covers the entire first floor of this big, early 1900s building, which exudes a leisurely, 1930s colonial ambience. The staff dress in black and white, the room is decorated in ice cream pink, and two large windows provide great views of Lord Street. On show inside you'll

find cream cakes, roulades and old-fashioned sponges, most of which are made in-house. You can choose from simple savouries like smoked salmon and scrambled eggs or bigger main courses. Some of the teas are organic and coffee from a good range is served by the cup, beaker or pot.

The 21-mile (34km) Sefton coastal footpath offers some wonderful sea views as it snakes from Southport to Crosby.

Truffles of Stamford

16 St. Mary's Hill, Stamford, Lincolnshire
Mon 10am–5pm, Tues, Thurs–Sat 9.30am–5pm, Sun 10.30am–4pm

As the name suggests, Truffles is principally a shop selling fine chocolates (mostly Belgian), but the selection of teas comes a close second. A scattering of tables occupies the small, cheerful shop (in an 18th-century building) and sweet foods are offered – around

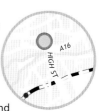

ten cakes on show, plus pastries and waffles. A special cream tea adds a slice of cake to two scones with whipped cream. The choice of loose-leaf teas ranges from Oolong and Russian

Caravan to tisanes, such as lavender. There are ten varieties of speciality coffee, served in cafetières, and the special hot chocolate is made to a secret recipe. Packaged tea and coffee is also sold.

"Tea, although an Oriental, is a gentleman at least; cocoa is a cad and coward, cocoa is a vulgar beast." **G.K. Chesterton (1874–1936)**

Chuzzlewits

26 Upgate, Louth, Lincolnshire
Tues–Sat 10am–4.30pm

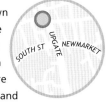

In the centre of this busy market town you'll find a local institution – the enormously popular and family-run Chuzzlewits, brimming with Victorian charm and elegance. The food and service are outstanding, thanks to Susan Westerman and her son who have run the business for eight years and are passionate about it. They shop early every morning to find the freshest ingredients and use plenty of organic produce.

All their cakes are served with a fresh-fruit garnish and, like the scones, are baked by hand the old-fashioned way. The setting is a large light-filled Victorian room facing the street, its two big

As well as being the historic capital of the Lincolnshire Wolds (twinned with La Ferte-Bernard in France), Louth is also unique in

windows decorated with vases of fresh flowers. The courteous staff dress in black and white, and on Saturdays wear Victorian-style garb. The tea is supplied by Taylors of Harrogate, the most popular choices being the loose-leaf China Rose Petal (black China tea layered with dried rose petals) and the Wild Cherry (also from China).

Food is served all day from brunch onwards and the imaginative sandwich selection includes bagels. Cream tea consists of a pot of tea served with a fruit scone, whipped cream and strawberry preserve. The traditional afternoon tea offers additional finger sandwiches and cake.

Alternatively, why not try a Fat Rascal – a cross between a rock bun and a scone, originating from the moorland areas near Whitby.

Susan and her husband also run an organic craft bakery, Babbits, which stocks a huge range of speciality teas and coffees. It is located nearby, opposite the Visitor Information Centre.

being a town in two hemispheres – east and west, as the Greenwich Meridian of zero degrees longitude passes through it.

Pimento Tea Rooms

26–27 Steep Hill, Lincoln, Lincolnshire
Mon–Sat 10am–5pm, Sun 10.30am–5pm

People travel from miles around to take tea at Pimento, which has been owned by Lesley Clarke for ten years. It occupies three levels of an 18th-century building above Imperial Teas of Lincoln, purveyors of fine teas and coffees from around the world, who are sole suppliers to the tea rooms. Over 250 teas are on sale here, as well as around 50 coffees. And to prove how exclusive Pimento really is, this is the only shop in the UK to stock one of the rarest of all teas, Jun Shan Silver Needles (a Chinese green tea). Produced in the Mount Jun area in Hunan province, only the buds are used to produce this sweet-tasting mellow tea.

On the top floor of the tea rooms, the quiet Pimento Parlour presents a wonderful view of the charming pedestrianized Steep Hill, and you're encouraged to relax with a supply of newspapers and magazines. It also houses an attractive coffee

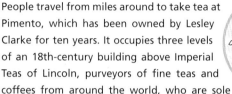

Lincoln has been awarded a £3 million European grant to build a new County and City Museum. To be completed by the end of 2003, the

roaster, which is still in use. The first floor contains three other pleasant rooms, each elegantly furnished.

The tea selection is the broadest you're likely to find – 23 varieties of loose-leaf, including green teas and rare connoisseurs' teas, such as Darjeeling Champagne Oolong, and wholefruit infusions. They are all served in individual glass teapots with their own infusers, while a helpful menu describes each tea in detail and recommends brewing times.

Coffee is roasted and ground on the premises from a choice of 15 varieties (including Hawaiian Kona) and served in cafetières, while the delicious hot chocolate comes with whipped cream and Amoretti biscuits.

All the food is vegetarian (some of it vegan), and the cakes and scones are made with free-range eggs. Light meals are listed daily on the specials board, and children's portions are available.

museum will be built next to the Usher Gallery in Danesgate and act as a gateway to the city's historic area that surrounds the cathedral.

Marples

6 Seaview St, Cleethorpes, Lincolnshire
Mon–Fri 9am–4.30pm, Sat 9am–5pm, Sun 9.30am–5pm

You'll find Marples just off the seafront. Husband-and-wife team Sheila and Dave Allen own this big glass-fronted tea room, which has a fresh, modern feel even though the building dates from the 1920s and the staff wear black-and-white uniforms. This place 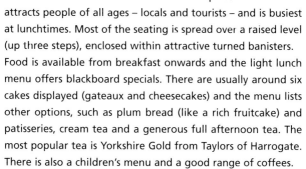 attracts people of all ages – locals and tourists – and is busiest at lunchtimes. Most of the seating is spread over a raised level (up three steps), enclosed within attractive turned banisters. Food is available from breakfast onwards and the light lunch menu offers blackboard specials. There are usually around six cakes displayed (gateaux and cheesecakes) and the menu lists other options, such as plum bread (like a rich fruitcake) and patisseries, cream tea and a generous full afternoon tea. The most popular tea is Yorkshire Gold from Taylors of Harrogate. There is also a children's menu and a good range of coffees.

Get out and about and explore the sand dunes, saltmarshes and mud flats at Cleethorpes' Humber Estuary Discovery Centre.

Northern Tea Merchants

Crown House, 193 Chatsworth Road, Chesterfield, Derbyshire
Mon–Sat 9am–5pm

A family business set up in 1959, this is chiefly a shop built in 1890 that sells fine teas and coffees, but it has bar counters where you can sit and sample the goods. Coffee roasting, tea blending and bagging take place elsewhere in the building; all the tea is bought direct from the growers. A gorgeous aroma greets you on entering this mellow, unpretentious and friendly shop – a sort of reference library for tea lovers. The food is limited to simple cakes and pastries, but the aim is to extend to all sorts of home-made goodies. Choose from 30 or so loose-leaf teas and as many coffees.

The owner, David Pogson, is a millionaire who chooses to continue working at the business he built up and still loves.

The Cottage Tea Room

3 Fennel Street, Ashford-in-the-Water, Derbyshire
Easter to end Sept, Sat–Mon, Wed & Thurs 2.30–5pm. Hours vary with seasons

For more than two decades the gregarious Bill Watkins has owned this teashop, for most of that time running it with his wife Betty. Since becoming a widower he has kept up the good work, serving the children of customers he first met as students, but these days he sticks to afternoon tea only. A founder member of the Tea Council, Bill certainly knows a thing or two about tea and

he offers an excellent range of loose-leaf and herbal infusions. He has also produced his own house blend and extra hot water is always served. The coffee is good, too, ground from a selection of beans including

Ashford-in-the-Water's 17th-century Sheepwash Bridge crosses the River Wye. The narrow packhorse bridge has a

120

Guatemalan Rainforest Coban and Brazilian Santos.

The 18th-century cottage is found near Sheepwash Bridge in this unspoilt Peak District village. You step into a cheery room, which is simply furnished but homely. The fireplace surround is made from local stone and dotted with fossils. The majority of customers are locals (one lady has visited the tea rooms every Thursday for 20 years) and tourists, while students love it, especially in the winter when they're hiking and potholing.

Bill does all the baking, creating the lightest dainty scones (try the herb ones, made with cheese on top) and a range of tasty cakes. The menu offers a range of full and light afternoon teas at good prices, but you're free to opt for just a slice of cake and a drink if you wish. The Derbyshire cream tea gives you three warm scones with whipped cream and jam, and a slice of cake. Bill is also happy to accommodate all sorts of dietary needs. The shop is especially busy when nearby Chatsworth House in Bakewell is open (mid-March to late December).

stone enclosure that was once used as a pen for holding sheep prior to being dipped (washed) in the river, thus explaining the name.

Ollerton Mill

Market Place, Ollerton, near Newark, Nottinghamshire
March till Oct, Tues–Sun 10.30am–5pm; Nov, Tues–Sun 10.30am–4pm. NB Please phone to check

In the centre of this pretty village on the edge of Sherwood Forest is the only water-powered mill in Nottinghamshire that's still operating, albeit as a museum. By the River Maun, it was built in 1713 on the site of a mill recorded in the Domesday Book and has

been restored to its former glory. On your way to the teashop on the first floor you pass the massive iron axle that turns the wheel (all the original machinery is intact) and can watch

the water race below you through a small glass panel in the floor. Owned by the same family since 1921, the mill houses an outstanding teashop in the millwright's workshop, opened in 1993

Set in the heart of Robin Hood country, and once one of the great private estates in Sherwood Forest, the nearby Rufford

by two sisters-in-law, Kate and Ellen Mettam. The atmosphere is friendly and light, with the brick walls painted white and a window at the back giving a view of the river. White tables, each with a small vase of fresh flowers, contribute to the sense of illumination. Above you are sturdy oak crossbeams.

Kate and Ellen do all the baking together in the tiny kitchen and they manage to produce several generous cakes, desserts and delicious scones every day. The cream tea brings you three scones, beautifully presented – dusted with icing sugar and accompanied by whipped cream and jam. The menu offers plenty of savoury snacks and light meals, such as the Ollerton Miller's Special – two types of cheese, apple, pickle, salad and a fresh roll. The list of speciality teas includes Jasmine, Rose Pouchong and Lady Grey. Coffee is served by the pot, cup or mug.

Country Park houses the picturesque remains of 12th-century Rufford Abbey. The park also has a craft centre and rose garden.

Bird on the Rock

Between Abcott and Clungunford, near Craven Arms, Shropshire

May to end Oct, Wed–Sun 10am–6pm; Nov to April, Wed–Sun 10am–5pm

Douglas and Annabel Hawkes opened this quintessential teashop in 1999 and haven't looked back. Together they have created a work of art. Taking their inspiration from the golden years of the 1920s and 30s, they have produced a teashop redolent with atmosphere and style. In an unspoilt, early 17th-century house

(Welsh longhouse design) are two tranquil beamed rooms decorated with a wealth of period objects and ephemera. The tables are set with blue and white Spode china and the staff dress in 1930s-style outfits. Tea is brought in stainless steel teapots that have their own infusers inside. Wood-burning stoves are lit in both rooms in

Bird on the Rock was one of only 12 Tea Council Guild members to have been judged worthy of special recognition

winter. In warm weather you can sit outside in the small, romantic English cottage garden with its picket fence border. The best ingredients are used for the food, inviting and utilizing as much local produce as possible. Douglas and Annabel make all their own cakes, bread and scones as well the preserves and conserves. They also keep a supply of gluten-free cakes and scones. Most of the tea is loose-leaf and you have a range of more than 40 to mull over, including organic and some of the teashop's own blends, such as Bertie's Brew (a lightly flavoured tea with a hint of cherry). The highest quality

teas are sourced, but all varieties are sold at the same price. Teas packaged by hand are also available. "We don't care how you take your tea, as long as you do it with style," says Douglas. Owing to the huge popularity of this teashop, it's best to book ahead at weekends, for a visit at any time of day. From July to September you need to book during the week as well.

n the Tea Council's 2002 Award of Excellence – assuring you of an ultimate tea experience. (Closed Tue and Wed after a bank holiday.)

Ann Boleyn's

Smallwood Lodge, 45 Upper Bar, Newport, Shropshire
Mon–Sat 9am–4pm, Sun 9am–11am

This distinctive building dates back to around 1600 and houses a teashop by day and a fully licensed restaurant by night (from Tuesday to Saturday). It's a focal point on the town's main street, especially with the small knot garden at the front. The premises have been sympathetically restored and decorated by the owners, Roy Stephenson and Owen Lavelle, the latter being an interior designer who has managed

to create a refined yet deeply relaxing space.

The tea and coffee are specially blended for Ann Boleyn's, the coffee being exceptionally smooth and free of bitterness, served

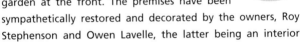

Ten miles (16km) from Newport are Hodnet Hall Gardens in the village of Market Drayton. Explore over 60 acres (24ha

by the cup or in a cafetière. The food is high quality and reasonably priced. These tea rooms are well known for the cream teas, presented on a tiered ceramic cake stand (with either whipped or clotted

cream). The local baker does all the baking and the locally home-made jam comes in various flavours, including the seldom seen greengage. The salads also have wide appeal, such as roasted salmon with basil oil dressing, as do the delicious soups. There are several main courses to choose from, and there's a separate menu for children.

Take your pick between two soothing wood-panelled tea rooms on the ground floor and seating in the front garden, which was designed by Owen. Further relaxation can be enjoyed in a small lounge area near the stairs, with windows dressed in sumptuous antique velvet. Attention to detail is clearly a priority here, so you'll find the tables dressed with linen tablecloths and sugar bowls carrying tongs. Roy and Owen also run an interior design business in Shrewsbury.

of magnificent forest trees, ornamental shrubs and flowers, with woodland walks alongside a chain of pools and lakes.

Leanne's Tea Rooms

13 Manor Walk, Market Harborough, Leicestershire
Mon–Fri 9am–5pm, Sat 9am–6pm, Sun 2–5pm

 V BH

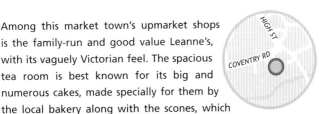

Among this market town's upmarket shops is the family-run and good value Leanne's, with its vaguely Victorian feel. The spacious tea room is best known for its big and numerous cakes, made specially for them by the local bakery along with the scones, which are served warm. Cream tea and afternoon tea are other specialities. The rest of the food is made on the premises

and vegetarians are catered to daily with at least two dishes. An extensive breakfast menu is followed by an equally broad range of snacks and cooked meals. The loose teas are Assam, Jasmine and Ceylon and there are a few organic varieties.

A baby grand piano is played every Tuesday and Friday – usually from 11am to 2pm – with mainly classical choices, but some requests

The Tea & Coffee Shop

33 Orford Place, Norwich, Norfolk
Mon–Sat 9am–4.30pm

A great city-centre teashop set above a shop selling fine teas, coffees and accessories. This modern first-floor room is a short stroll from the city's market – the biggest six-day outdoor market in the country (Mon–Sat). The great range of teas, all loose-leaf (32), extends to green teas. The Assams and strong Breakfast blends are brewed in tap water; all the others in filtered water.

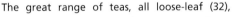

The coffee is freshly ground and you can choose from 18 beans and 11 blends. All the food is made in-house, featuring naturally cured ham, omelettes and Welsh rarebit, alongside daily specials. On display are generous cakes, gateaux and fruit pies, always including gluten-free choices.

When visiting Norwich make sure you try the famous Aldous ice cream, made the traditional way – with milk.

Ye Olde Tea Room

Song of the Surf, 7 Lifeboat Plain (off Gun Street), Sheringham, Norfolk

April–Oct, Tues–Sun 10.30am–5pm (closed Mon); Nov–March, Thurs–Sun 11am–4pm

A stone's throw from a sandy beach lies this small, family-run, traditional teashop in the holiday town of Sheringham. It occupies the ground floor of a flint cottage built in 1850, modernized inside and evocatively named Song of the Surf. The yesteryear atmosphere is

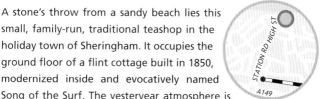

enhanced by 1950s band music, played in the background and complemented by a wooden Bush radio of the same period. All the cakes are made in the shop (around five available daily)

and cream tea is served with whipped cream. A speciality is Sheringham crab, freshly caught that day by their local fisherman, and the menu offers snacks and light lunches, as well as organic fruit juices. Tea and coffee are served with free top-ups.

Market days are Saturday and Wednesday, the latter being the town's half-day closing day, but the teashop stays open if busy enough.

The Aristocrat Tearooms

5 Bond Street, Cromer, Norfolk

June to Sept, Tues–Sat 9.30am–7pm, Sun 10.30am–3pm. Hours vary with seasons

Paul Godfrey has worked in catering all his life, and it shows in the quality of service in the traditional teashop he owns with his wife, Valerie. Located in the heart of the seaside town, near the Church of St Peter and St Paul, it has a friendly atmosphere, a strong following of locals and a sheltered sunny patio at the rear. All the tea is supplied by Ashbys, around six types of cake

are offered daily, and cream tea is served in summer. A speciality here is Cromer crab, but the menu also gives a dish of the day and a good-value set lunch menu of two or three courses, which changes daily.

Cromer overlooks some of Norfolk's sandiest beaches, and the town's unique museum is located in a row of small fishermen's cottages.

Margaret's Tea Room

Chestnut Farmhouse, The Street, Baconsthorpe, near Holt, Norfolk
March to end Oct, Tues–Sun 10.30am–5pm; Nov to mid-Dec, weekends only 10.30am–5pm

On the main street of this pretty, flintstone Norfolk village just outside Holt is a cheery traditional teashop in a 17th-century farmhouse. Owned since 1992 by Margaret and Roger Bacon, it has won the Tea Council's Award of Excellence in 1997, 1998, 2001 and 2002. These tea rooms are renowned for attention to detail and outstanding food, all made by Margaret, who starts

baking at an ungodly hour each day. Her cakes are hearty, her scones among the best you'll ever taste (try the toasted cheese and herb scone), made to a secret recipe and served warm

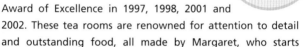

Reached by a maze of tiny lanes in rural countryside are the enigmatic ruins of Baconsthorpe Castle, managed by English

with whipped local cream and her home-made preserves. Light lunches include soups, salads, flans and delicious quiches, such as stilton, apricot and walnut quiche with home-made walnut bread and salad. Desserts include shortbreads, strawberry meringues, and a selection of ice cream flavours.

When it comes to beverages, take your pick from an excellent range of 25 teas (most of them loose-leaf) such as Formosa Oolong and Pai Mu Tan (rare Chinese white tea), all brewed in removable infusion bags and served in bone china. A pot for one will provide you with at least four cups' worth. Ten varieties of freshly ground coffee are available, served by the cafetière. Choose where to sit and enjoy yourself in one of two parlours or the delightful lawned garden at the front.

With its beautiful decor, dainty tea sets and some lovely pieces of furniture, it's not difficult to see why Margaret's Tea Rooms deserve their prize-winning reputation.

Heritage. Dating from the 15th century, the castle was built by the Heydon family as both a manor house and wool-processing factory.

"There are few hours in life more agreeable than the hour dedicated to the ceremony known as afternoon tea."

Henry James (1843–1916)

Wales

Oscars

High Town, Hay-on-Wye, Powys/Herefordshire border
Easter to mid-Sept, daily 10.30am–5.30pm. Hours vary with seasons

This 18th-century building has two rooms furnished with simple wooden tables, bentwood chairs and church pews. Counter service is provided in the busier ground-floor room, while the first floor provides a retreat, and outdoor tables are placed on Market Street.

This is a popular lunchtime venue, the good-value food being made on the premises from local ingredients to include beef

and ale pies, plenty of snacks and main courses, and a good selection of pastries and desserts, such as German apple cake. Decaffeinated tea is available and coffee is served by the cup or cafetière from three types of bean.

Hay, or 'Booktown' as it is known, has over 40 bookshops and is home to the world's biggest literary festival, held annually in May.

Badgers Café & Patisserie

The Victoria Centre (shopping mall), Mostyn Street, Llandudno, Gwynedd
Mon–Sat 9.30am–5pm, Sun 11am–4pm

Since its opening in 1997, Badgers has been managed by Donna Goodrich. Whittards supply all the tea and coffee, the loose-leaf speciality teas offering such variety as Keemun (a delicate China tea) and Assam Harmutty (a rare flowery Orange Pekoe). Choose your cafetière coffee from an impressive range of beans including a couple of rare ones. The resident master bakers work all day to produce a range of enticing patisseries,

wheeled to your table by staff dressed in Victorian-style outfits. Other specialities are traditional Welsh rarebit and a choice of afternoon teas, such as Welsh cream tea in which a slice of Bara Brith accompanies the scone.

"Better to be deprived of food for three days than tea for one."
Ancient Chinese proverb

Cemlyn

High Street, Harlech, Gwynedd
Easter to end Oct, Tues–Sun 11am–4pm (closed Mon)

 V BH ♟

The outstanding Cemlyn is run by Jan and Geoff Cole, who put every effort into ensuring a memorable visit. Regulars come from as far as Caernarfon to select from the outstanding choice of loose-leaf teas – 21 options plus fruit and herbal infusions, and tisanes. You'll find such exotic varieties as Formosa Oolong (from the Far East), Nilgiri (from India) and South African

Rooibos (a red tea). The quality of coffee is superb, too, served by the cup or cafetière from three different types of bean, including Mexican Maragogype.

The elegant and uplifting surroundings are a delight:

 Sited on a rocky elevation 200ft (61m) above the shoreline of Tremadoc Bay is the formidable 13th-century Harlech Castle.

traditional linen tablecloths and comfortable upholstered chairs in a beautifully decorated, cheerful Edwardian room. It comes as no surprise, then, that the teashop becomes a smart restaurant in the evenings. The room is divided into two sections, the far end allowing views over the teashop's small terrace to Harlech Castle, Tremadoc Bay and, on a clear day, as far as Snowdon.

Nearly all the food is made in-house to extremely high standards and is sold at sensible, affordable prices. Cemlyn makes its own bread, is famous for its teacakes, uses Welsh buttermilk in the scones (as people did in Victorian times), and Belgian chocolate in its brownies. The teashop is also known for its Welsh rarebit (the real thing, with beer, mature Welsh cheese, and wholegrain mustard). Additional sweets offered are Bara Brith (traditional Welsh tea bread), farmhouse fruitcake, Eccles cake and, of course, Welsh cakes.

Once a powerful coastal defence, today the castle is still impressive, set against a backdrop of the magnificent Snowdonia range.

Felin Newydd

Crugybar, Llanwrda, Carmarthenshire
April till October, Thurs–Mon 10.30am–5pm. Open Tuesdays in July and August

The name means 'new mill', and regulars come from as far as Swansea, Cardiff, and Hereford and Worcester to enjoy the tranquillity of this hamlet. It's well off the beaten track, set in a beautiful emerald valley between the Cambrian Mountains, and contains a 300-year-old working watermill, so isn't quite as new as its name suggests. In the grounds you'll find a small teashop

that occupies an attractive, modern conservatory attached to a renovated byre (a craft shop today). The conservatory gives tremendous views over the lush 13-acre (5ha) gardens, which keep their bright green colour all year round, and

 A century ago mills such as Felin Newydd were found roughly every three miles (5km) along the Welsh river

140

towards the hills beyond. Three acres are open to the public, containing a wildlife pond, river and woodland (£1 entrance fee to gardens, but access to teashop is free; £2 for both the gardens and a self-tour inside the mill, which is sometimes switched on). You can enjoy a 40-minute loop walk beside the river or stroll along a section of it.

The extremely hospitable Chris and Jo-Anne Maple have owned the mill, gardens and teashop since 1999. Jo-Anne does all the cooking, making the most of eggs from their own chickens, vegetables from the garden, ham that they roast at home, and local produce such as organic cheese. She creates a generous range of cakes that includes lemon cheesecake, summer fruit tartlets and Welsh cakes, as well as a simple range of light lunches. The Miller's Tea offers two scones with Pembrokeshire clotted cream and all the usual trimmings. All the tea is loose-leaf, the speciality ones being Darjeeling, Assam, Earl Grey and Lapsang Souchong. Coffee comes in a cafetière.

valleys. Believed to be one of the oldest mill sites in Britain, today it is one of the last remaining water-powered corn mills in the area.

Gwalia Tea Rooms

Museum of Welsh Life, St Fagans, Glamorgan
Daily 10am–4.45pm

In the fascinating open-air Museum of Welsh Life, showing how the Welsh have lived during the last 500 years, over 40 original buildings have been moved from all parts of Wales and re-erected in the grounds of a 16th-century manor house called St Fagans Castle. Entry to the grounds and teashop is free although a charge is made for entry to the indoor galleries. Pick up the

informative visitor booklet at the entrance and a five-minute walk along the path brings you to the teashop. Along the way you'll pass the red Kennixton Farmhouse (a 1610 structure from southwest Wales, originally painted red to ward off evil spirits) and a bakehouse still in use,

The Museum of Welsh Life houses a vast range of buildings including a school, a chapel, a Workmen's Institute and

among other buildings. The Gwalia Tea Rooms are above the Gwalia Supply Co., a general store and ironmongers dating from 1880, which served its community for almost a century. Today confectionery and a few general provisions are still sold in one section.

The simple traditional teashop occupies the length of the first floor, accessed through a storeroom of tin baths and buckets and up a wooden staircase. The reasonably priced menu provides an excellent selection of speciality teas, most of them loose-leaf – China, Indian and Sri Lankan, African, and Russian. Cakes are made daily in the museum kitchen to traditional recipes using flour from the St Fagans mill. You'll find such offerings as Welsh cakes, Bara Brith (rich spiced fruit bread served with butter), Teisen Lap (light spicy fruit cake) and the Gwalia rock cake (slightly spiced and fruity). The Welsh rarebit is served on a slice of Swansea loaf with chutney.

everal workshops where craftsmen, such as the blacksmith nd the cooper, demonstrate their skills to the public.

"Never trust a man who, when he's alone in a room with a tea-cosy, doesn't try it on."

Billy Connolly

Scotland

The Willow Tea Rooms

217 Sauchiehall Street, Glasgow, Lanarkshire

Mon–Sat 9am–4.30pm, Sun midday–3.30pm (but closed Sun between New Year and Easter)

In 1903 the acclaimed architect Charles Rennie Mackintosh began work for teashop entrepreneur Kate Cranston (*see pp.148–149, Miss Cranston's*) to design and build one of several tea rooms that were constructed around this period. Today, located above a jewellers, the first floor of the Willow Tea Rooms houses the attractive Gallery while on the second floor is the Room de Luxe, with its silver furniture and mirror friezes.

Teas are all loose-leaf and the list extends to Gunpowder, Russian Caravan, and Kenya. The coffee is also great, served by the cup or cafetière, from a choice of four beans. An extensive breakfast menu is offered all day, as is Miss Cranston's special afternoon tea. The day's patisseries and cakes are also displayed. Savoury specialities are haggis, neeps and tatties, and Arbroath Smokie (smoked haddock).

The word Sauchiehall is derived from 'saugh', the Scots word for a willow tree, and 'haugh', the word for a meadow.

The Willow Tea Rooms

97 Buchanan Street, Glasgow, Lanarkshire

Daily 9am–5pm. Chinese Room is only open on Saturdays, during school holidays and at Christmas

Following the success of the Willow Tea Rooms on Sauchiehall Street, this sister shop opened in 1997, continuing the Willow name first used by Kate Cranston (*see* overleaf). It contains two sympathetic recreations: the White Dining Room (originally designed in 1900), and upstairs the vivid blue Chinese Room (*pictured, and first created in 1911*). The menu is identical to that of the

Sauchiehall Street premises, but it can get a little noisy here, owing to an espresso machine and the general teashop clatter. However, the great food and drink make it an experience well worth paying for.

> **"A woman is like a teabag – only in hot water do you realise how strong she is."**
> **Nancy Reagan**

Miss Cranston's

33 Gordon Street, Glasgow, Lanarkshire
Mon–Sat 8.30–5pm

You'll find this soothing space above a patisserie on Glasgow's Gordon Street. The teashop is named after Kate Cranston, who opened several successful establishments in the city at the end of the 19th century and start of the 20th. This contemporary venue is a fitting tribute, an elegant retreat created by two young Glasgow designers, Anne Perry and Karen Longmuir. Cream-coloured walls are decorated with tall panels etched with recipes and they make the most of the light that filters through the big windows. Linen tablecloths are paired with muted yellow upholstered chairs. Two corner windows meet to give good views of the street below, and wonderful aromas waft through from the family-run craft bakery (Bradfords), which owns the teashop. It produces delicious patisseries and breads, some made with organic flour.

Kate Cranston was born into a tea-importing family. She became famous for bringing designers like George Walton and Charles

Another boon is the loose-leaf tea, such as Japanese Sencha and Golden Ceylon. The coffee is also good, from four different types including the rich house blend – Miss Cranston's Deluxe – served by the

cup or cafetière. Renowned for its afternoon teas, Miss Cranston's gives you luxury sandwiches followed by scones and pancakes with cream and jam, plus fancy cream cakes. Any cakes you can't manage at the table can be boxed for you to take home. The Cream Tea Special is served in the morning (until 11.30am) and afternoon (after 2.30pm). Light breakfasts are available until midday; lunch mains include traditional Scotch pie cases with a selection of tasty fillings such as prime minced Aberdeen Angus beef. Lunchtime specials include the 'Quick Meal' of soup and sandwich, and a range of tasty open sandwiches. Speciality desserts include the famous handmade Cumnock tart (made to the same recipe and method since 1924). Children also have their own menu.

Rennie Mackintosh to the fore, whom she commissioned to design for her (see the Willow Tea Rooms, p.146 and p.147).

Kind Kyttock's Kitchen

Cross Wynd, Falkland, Fife
Tues–Sun 10.30am–5.30pm, and bank holiday Fridays

Kind Kyttock's Kitchen is signposted as a tourist attraction in its own right and has been run for many years by Bert Dalrymple, who does all the baking. Virtually all the food is produced in-house and there's a good supply of everything. Hot favourites are apple tart, fudge cake, and Clootie Dumplin' – a dumpling wrapped in a cloth (clootie) and boiled, served with a sweet sauce. The water is chlorine-free and makes a lovely cup of loose-leaf; the

coffee is freshly ground and served by the cup. The teashop occupies two simple rooms, one on the ground floor (with the original stone fireplace used in winter, and sash windows onto the street) and another above it.

Nearby Falkland Palace, built between 1501 and 1541, was the country residence of a total of eight Stuart monarchs.

Sir Walter Scott's

Above Romanes & Paterson, 62 Princes Street, Edinburgh, Midlothian
Mon–Sat 9am–5pm, Sun 10am–5pm

Owned by the Edinburgh Wool Mill, the popular and relaxed Sir Walter Scott's is on the second floor of a tall Victorian building that benefits from tremendous views over the impressive Princes Street Gardens. There's no missing the Scottish tradition here – the curtains and carpet are tartan, while shortbread, haggis and oatcakes are on the menu, along with the speciality Clootie

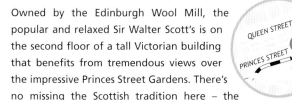

Dumplin' (like Christmas pudding and served warm with whipped cream). The Scottish afternoon tea gives you sandwiches, fruitcake and shortbread. All the food is produced in-house from ingredients such as free-range eggs and Scottish cheddar matured on Orkney. The tea is supplied by Twinings.

In the heart of Princes Street Gardens, the Scott Monument is a 200ft (61m) high memorial to one of Edinburgh's favourite sons.

Plaisir du Chocolat

251–253 Canongate (on the Royal Mile), Edinburgh, Midlothian
Tues, Wed & Sun 10am–6pm; Thurs–Sat 10am–10.30pm. Closed Mon

This peaceful haven on Edinburgh's Royal Mile is a treasure chest for any tea connoisseur or those willing to learn. It is run like a French salon but contains a café, an épicerie and a restaurant, and sells an astounding number of teas, nearly 180 in all. The menu lists them

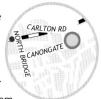

by region, giving evocative descriptions like 'The height of perfection in white tea' for the Chinese Yin Zhen (also known as Silver Needles), and many varieties are rare. The tea is made

with Scottish mineral water and most varieties are brewed before they reach the table. There are also several types of iced tea on offer. All the teas are also sold in the attached shop, along with coffee and

Edinburgh Castle has stood guard high over the city since 1085. A stroll down the Castle Esplanade affords visitors an unrivalled view

chocolate from all over the world. Creamy hot chocolate is another house speciality.

The serene environment is created by a stylish art nouveau interior design combined with the calm, efficient staff. Varying soft shades of green combine with ornate mirrors, exquisite lampshades of the period, high-backed wicker chairs and fresh lilies on the tables to help you to relax. Passing the excellent range of French patisseries on the way in is sure to whet your appetite. The head chef, Bertrand Espouy, is passionate about his work; the food is outstanding – traditional French, good value and all made on the premises from the best ingredients (plenty of organic), many of them brought in from France, such as bread from Paris. Beginning with breakfast, food is served through to afternoon tea and high tea, to include a wealth of savoury dishes. Why not enjoy a typically French *petit-déjeuner* of tea or hot chocolate with a brioche? Or an elegant high tea served with sandwiches, cakes and biscuits, brioche and petit fours? To dine at Plaisir du Chocolat means to indulge yourself.

of the cobblestoned streets of the Old Town, and the bustling activity of the city's financial sector, the New Town.

Coach House Coffee Shop

Loch Lomond & The Trossachs National Park, Luss, Argyll

Daily 10am–5pm (July & Aug till 6pm when busy)

The Coach House is located a short stroll from Loch Lomond in this delightfully pretty conservation village, which is the nucleus of the first national park to be established in Scotland. Although it is called a coffee shop, this place doubles as an excellent teashop. Rowena and Gary Groves (a warm host who wears a kilt every day) began this business in 1998. Building from scratch on the site of an old coach house, the couple have created a big, contemporary barn-like space furnished to reflect the

ruggedness of parts of Scotland. A high ceiling, bare wooden floors and a big stone fireplace (with a log fire in winter) all contribute to the feel. Outside there's a modest gravelled garden (dogs welcomed).

Loch Lomond & The Trossachs National Park encompasses around 720 square miles (1865sq km) of some of the finest scenery in

Huge numbers of tourists visit the village annually, but the teashop also sees plenty of day-trippers from Glasgow as well as locals, especially families. Apart from the house-blend tea bag tea (a classic blend of Assam, Kenya and Ceylon), the teas are loose-leaf. Included in the list are Keemun, Gunpowder and high-grown Ceylon. They also make their own iced tea, and the coffee menu is extensive.

Virtually all of the food is made in-house (a few of the gateaux are brought in), and it's all hearty, wholesome fare. House specialities are shortbread, generous scones, which are served warm (the apple and cinnamon ones have chunks of apple in them), and delicious stokies – huge filled rolls. Other specialities are apple pie, bread and butter pudding (with lemon rind instead of spices) and Orkney ice cream. Rowena and Gary also roast their own hams and use free-range eggs in all of the cooking. On winter days several varieties of home-made soup are offered, served in huge bowls. The Coach House also has a policy to try and accommodate the majority of dietary needs.

Scotland. Lowland landscapes in the south contrast with the towering mountains of the north, with lochs, rivers and woodland in between.

155

Index

Page numbers are shown in **bold**.

Acknowledgements

Laura Harper would like to thank Tony Mudd for all his encouragement and guidance – and for creating the Tip-top series; all the staff at Studio Cactus, but especially Aaron Brown for his diligence, patience and good humour in editing and overseeing the project; Sharon Moore and Laura Watson for making every effort to produce such a pleasing design; and Mandy Lunn and Damien Moore for having the faith to back the series in the first place. Finally, thanks to the members of the public who recommended their favourite teashop by radio, letter or email – we couldn't have done it without you!

Studio Cactus would like to thank David Ashby for creating the maps.

Picture Credits
Corbis: Front jacket; Hulton Getty: 9, 10; Anthony Blake Picture Library: 6
All other photos by Laura Harper and Tony Mudd

Also in this series...

If you love fish and chips then you'll love this title, the only guide dedicated to **Britain's favourite fast food**.

Tip-top

FISH & CHIP SHOPS
England's Top 100 fish and chip shops

Tony Mudd

"Fascinating... crammed full of information, including location maps, opening hours, and local specialities."

Daily Express